D0288222

"Daniel Lohrmann offers a splendid survey of the many benefits and drawbacks of cyber-technologies. Parents, pastors, and employers will gain 'virtual' wisdom amidst today's ethical quandaries."

—**Quentin J. Schultze**, Calvin College

"Dan Lohrmann is a leader in the information security field and his extensive knowledge is demonstrated throughout the book. Protecting ourselves from the dangers that lurk in cyberspace has to be a multi-faceted approach. *Virtual Integrity* describes one approach in depth and challenges us on how to explore cyberspace safely. Lohrmann offers his insight and passion to his readers, and is an excellent role model."

—**William Pelgrin**, chair of the Multi-State Information Sharing and Analysis Center

"Lohrmann reminds us that integrity on the Internet involves more than purchasing a family friendly filter. He wisely connects virtual with embodied reality, challenges us to 'surf our values,' and then packs his book with practical ways to do just that. This book inspires and empowers us to bring every corner of our virtual world under the Lordship of Christ."

—**Michael Wittmer**, Grand Rapids Theological Seminary

"*Virtual Integrity* succeeds on three important levels—personal, corporate, and national. Written by a person of solid professional credentials and proven integrity, this book is a roadmap for the future of the Internet. The Internet still is, and will continue to be, the Wild West. No government is going to control it, so it is up to us as individuals to protect ourselves. However, we as individuals need tools to do that; Lohrmann provides those tools clearly and concisely. More important, *Virtual Integrity* offers a solid roadmap, grounded in universal truths, for corporations and governments alike. You don't need to be a Christian to benefit tremendously from Lohrmann's book."

—**Peter Stephenson**, chief information security officer and associate director of the Master of Science in Information Assurance program, Norwich University

"*Virtual Integrity* is a book that should be read by every parent, teacher, church worker . . . everyone using the Internet. This book will pose many questions concerning your use of the Internet; you will be introduced to a whole new language and set of challenges. But *Virtual Integrity* also offers solutions. Lohrmann teaches us that, as Christians, we have the responsibility to navigate the virtual world with the same values we use in the real world."

—**Lindsay Conway**, secretary to the Presbyterian Board
of Social Witness and director of Social Service
(Presbyterian Church in Ireland)

VIRTUAL INTEGRITY

Faithfully Navigating the Brave New Web

DANIEL J. LOHRMANN

BrazosPress

a division of Baker Publishing Group
Grand Rapids, Michigan

© 2008 by Daniel J. Lohrmann

Published by Brazos Press
a division of Baker Publishing Group
P.O. Box 6287, Grand Rapids, MI 49516–6287
www.brazospress.com

Printed in the United States of America

All rights reserved. No part of this publication may be reproduced, stored in a retrieval system, or transmitted in any form or by any means—for example, electronic, photocopy, recording—without the prior written permission of the publisher. The only exception is brief quotations in printed reviews.

Library of Congress Cataloging-in-Publication Data
Lohrmann, Daniel J., 1963—
    Virtual integrity : faithfully navigating the brave new web / Daniel J. Lohrmann.
      p.   cm.
    Includes bibliographical references. (p.   ).
    ISBN 978-1-58743-234-7 (pbk.)
    1. Internet—Religious aspects—Christianity. 2. Internet—Moral and ethical aspects.
  3. Christian ethics. I. Title
  BR99.74.L67 2008
  241′.65—dc22
                                                   2008020170

Scripture marked ESV is taken from The Holy Bible, English Standard Version, copyright © 2001 by Crossway Bibles, a division of Good News Publishers. Used by permission. All rights reserved.

Scripture marked NIV is taken from the HOLY BIBLE, NEW INTERNATIONAL VERSION®. NIV®. Copyright © 1973, 1978, 1984 by International Bible Society. Used by permission of Zondervan. All rights reserved.

Scripture marked NKJV is taken from the New King James Version. Copyright © 1982 by Thomas Nelson, Inc. Used by permission. All rights reserved.

Scripture marked NRSV is taken from the New Revised Standard Version of the Bible, copyright 1989, Division of Christian Education of the National Council of the Churches of Christ in the United States of America. Used by permission. All rights reserved.

BR99.74
.L67
2008

In keeping with biblical principles of creation stewardship, Baker Publishing Group advocates the responsible use of our natural resources. As a member of the Green Press Initiative, our company uses recycled paper when possible. The text paper of this book is comprised of 30% post-consumer waste.

green press
INITIATIVE

0216937329

This book is dedicated to my father, Enno Karl Lohrmann (1924–88). I am eternally grateful for his words of encouragement. My dad modeled excellence and integrity in sports, marriage, faith, and family.

To my mother, Marguerite C. Lohrmann, whose prayers have made success possible and strengthened me through every trial. Your zeal for God and perseverance for family never cease to amaze me. I am so thankful for your love and faithfulness.

To my precious wife, Priscilla. You are such a wonderful gift from heaven! You motivate and challenge me in so many ways. Thank you for being a wonderful mother, a beautiful spouse, and my best friend. I love you more each day.

To Grace, Katherine, Paul, and Lydia. Being your father brings me special joy! You are such a special blessing and gift from above. I pray that each of you will faithfully navigate the brave new Web and live as Christians with integrity.

 # Contents

Acknowledgments   9

Introduction   11

1. Integrity Theft: *How e-Temptation Targets You*   17
2. Why Filtering Is Not Enough: *Problems with Parental Controls*   31
3. Who's Fooling Whom in Cyberspace? *Overcoming Online Deception*   45
4. Do the Ends Justify the Means? *Cheating on the Web*   63
5. Identity Theft and Integrity Theft: *Partners in Crime*   77
6. This Is Looking Like Work: *How Cyber Ethics Impact Your Business and Career*   97
7. Just Do It: *Creating and Maintaining Virtual Integrity*   119
8. Surf Your Values: *More Habits to Keep Integrity Going*   139
9. What If? *2012, a Cyberspace Odyssey*   169
10. Brave New Web: *A Flood of Questions*   189

Appendix: Toward a New National Strategy on Cyber Ethics   201

Notes   211

➜ Acknowledgments

I never could have written this book without the help of several wonderful friends and professional supporters. I would like to thank my wife, Priscilla, who constantly questions my perspectives and attitude toward computers and the Internet.

Rodney Clapp, my primary Brazos editor, has been nothing short of an angel for this first-time author who rambles. Lisa Ann Cockrel kept me on the straight and narrow while patiently answering all my questions. BJ Heyboer, Lauren Forsythe, and everyone else at Brazos were truly remarkable.

Dr. Dorothy Bass provided early connections and direction, Dr. Marsha Daigle-Williamson steered my writing focus, and David Gilliland offered technical insights. Last but not least, Brian Flowerday and Pastor Brian McLaughlin challenged me to clarify my recommendations.

➡ Introduction

I do not pray for success, I ask for faithfulness.

Mother Teresa of Calcutta[1]

Tim excelled at work, and his colleagues and staff trusted him. But one day Tim's executive assistant accidentally discovered that he was running a questionable online business during office hours. For weeks, Agnes tried to ignore her boss's behavior, but she couldn't live with herself. Agnes anonymously reported him to security. Once caught, Tim lied to cover up his activities. When faced with undeniable evidence, he blamed others. One lie led to another until he was deemed untrustworthy. Tim resigned just before he was fired.

The names are changed, yet stories similar to this happen every day in America. From new employees at small businesses to executives at America's largest corporations, a new e-morality is emerging. While thousands crash and burn each year because of surfing the Internet inappropriately at home or work, the vast majority of the tragedies never make the evening news. These are some of America's best and brightest, the ones who should know better.

What happens next? Some people learn from their mistakes and reform their ways. Others resume their online misdeeds after just a few months of good behavior at their new job. Many times, the cycle of unacceptable behavior repeats itself at the new employer.

(For legal reasons, cyber indiscretions become forever sealed in human resources files that can't be shared.)

As Michigan's Chief Information Security Officer and the Director of Enterprise Security within the Department of Information Technology, I oversee an office that monitors and secures sensitive government information and protects Internet access for over 50,000 government employees. Through coordinated work with other states, the federal government, local municipalities across the United States, the private sector, and law enforcement organizations worldwide, we have access and insight into the global Internet activities that impact hundreds of millions of users each day. Our Michigan security team has been recognized as one of the best in the technology industry.

Over the past twenty-four years, I've led teams building award-winning websites and customer-focused portals that have changed the way citizens and businesses interact with government—for the better. Since working for the National Security Agency (NSA) in the 1980s, I've circled the globe fixing computers, battling hackers, stopping computer viruses, and taking on a never-ending list of "bad guys." While working for Mantech in northern England in the 1990s, I directed the Network Management Group (NMG) that ran networks for the U.S. Department of Defense (DoD) and the U.K. Ministry of Defense (MoD). America still faces serious challenges from foreign threats, and many books have been written and websites developed on all aspects of cybersecurity, organized crime, and protecting your confidential information. I've seen firsthand a lot of these threats and abuses of Internet capabilities. But recently an even more troubling trend has grabbed my attention.

A set of digital problems has emerged that is more daunting than stopping organized cyber crime or addressing Internet privacy. A related, but cleverly veiled, set of attacks with new names is wreaking havoc on families. Even when all the right defenses are in place, I still see too many among the supposed "good guys" surfing inappropriately and destructively. Young and old are enticed into performing actions that sacrifice their future. Increasingly, I see the ethical and moral lines in cyberspace becoming blurry for large parts of our society and even most churchgoers.

As a husband, a father of four, and a committed Christian who teaches children and adults at our church, I've watched as a subtle, yet powerfully growing, number of appeals try harder than ever to undermine my purpose-driven life. These assaults threaten my faith, my personal reputation, my marriage, my children, my career, and even the effectiveness of my entire department at work. Since nothing is new under the sun, I'm not suggesting that these attacks are entirely unprecedented. However, I do believe PCs, mobile computing, cell phones, BlackBerries, and the millions of things we can do on the Internet have forever changed the scope and sophistication of the battles that we face in the twenty-first century.

Specifically, I am referring to an extraordinary increase in the number of temptations we face in cyberspace. New seductions are cleverly packaged as "innovative opportunities" that are really appeals to engage in unproductive, harmful, and even immoral activities online. A much wider set of questions has arisen that can't be answered by simply blocking spam, installing Web filters, or upgrading your antivirus software and PC firewall. These virtual threats can have the net effect of taking away some of the most important things in life. As individuals, institutions, and a nation, we spend significant time battling identity theft online, but we neglect to fight other negative aspects of Internet life that I call "integrity theft." We need a new approach to virtual integrity.

This book is the result of several years of research regarding common Internet behavior around the country. I have deep concerns, but I'm certainly not in favor of abandoning the Internet and trashing our computers. There are millions of good (and great) things to do online. From checking weather to shopping to reading e-mail to doing research, using the Internet has become a way of life in the Lohrmann household. So my focus is on how to improve, not remove, our virtual experiences. How can we bolster the likelihood of doing the "right" things and stop doing the "wrong" things? Bottom line, is it possible to surf our values? I'm confident that the answer is yes, but we all need help—and not just from technology companies. The solutions need to start with our beliefs and values. Faithful navigation of the brave new Web involves changes in people and processes, as well as technology.

The Goal—A Cyber Roadmap for Christian Living

You may be thinking: Is this really such a big problem? Aren't you overstating the importance of our Internet actions? I think not, but I recognize the need to show you why. In the opening chapter of this book, I define integrity theft and describe the full measure of its effects. I show what I mean by genuine integrity and discuss why it is so essential for Christians to opt in, in order to surf one's values at home, school, and work.

Chapter 2 addresses the need for a new mind-set regarding Web filters and blocking content with parental controls. While current techniques can be helpful, protections are drastically oversold. We need to address answers in terms of people, processes, and technology solutions that are portable. I make the case that our exclusive focus on child protections may actually be hindering the moral environment for adults online. Many families are trying their best, but where can they go for more help? I provide answers, helpful tools, and strategies that you can use right now.

Chapters 3–5 describe our current situation in more depth, with real-life stories and an emphasis on how people are getting into trouble by renaming activities that equate to lying, cheating, stealing, and lust. These chapters show how many security and privacy problems are really moral and ethical issues at their root. I provide many examples of how the online world is rapidly changing—making it difficult to keep up with the latest technical issues. The right habits can bring success if we learn to stop, think, and click, with a technically savvy biblical mind-set. I also provide recommendations and guidance in each area.

In chapter 6, I shift gears and address the relevance of this topic at work and in career advancement. Surfing your values at the office is growing into a huge issue for the global economy. In fact, cyber ethics will become a top issue for companies worldwide over the next few years. I challenge Christians to examine their actions at work, not just from a "top-down" corporate ethics or a policy-compliance perspective, but from a perspective of biblically based obedience and faithfulness.

In chapters 7 and 8, I'll walk you step by step down a path to faithfully navigate the brave new Web with seven habits of online integrity. As you will see, these seven habits include choosing and applying the right technology (habit four), but are even more centrally a matter of learning how to put our real values to work in cyberspace (the other six habits).

In chapters 9 and 10, I ask "what if" things were different. As the Internet develops, more and more personalization of what we see will develop. I take you on a journey to the near future and demonstrate how new technology can revolutionize our Internet experiences and allow us to surf our values in powerful, exciting new ways. Just as our shopping preferences currently tailor what ads are presented to us on the Web, our integrity, our spirituality, and our morality can also tailor what comes to us over the Web. If Christians and others who want to surf their values rise up and demand this functionality, it will be provided.

To accomplish this vision, change will be required by more than just individuals. Just as doctors have long subscribed to the Hippocratic Oath, the technology industry needs to rethink the ethics of what they're doing to society. In the appendix, I've outlined practical steps toward a new national strategy for cyber ethics, which include tasks for individuals, churches, businesses, governments, and for the IT and media industries that produce and deliver content. We can't keep doing the same thing and expect a different result.

All Things Are Possible

If surfing your values seems like an impossible task, I agree—in purely worldly terms. We need heavenly help. Psalm 121:1–2 says "I lift up my eyes to the hills—where does my help come from? My help comes from the LORD, the Maker of heaven and earth" (NIV). This is a personal battle that you cannot win without God's help. I believe prayer, scripture, and regular Christian fellowship are all essential elements to winning this online moral battle. We can also benefit from the wisdom of great Christian leaders, so all along the way I will point you toward a variety of helpful books, websites, and other resources.

Today's Internet culture constantly entices us to water down the Ten Commandments, forget God's promises, justify questionable actions, and live in cyber shades of gray. But rather than withdraw, we can boldly move forward with confidence and integrity. Please join me in digging deeper into building genuine integrity into virtual life and redeeming your cyberspace.

1 ➡ Integrity Theft

How e-Temptation Targets You

And lead us not into temptation, but deliver us from evil.

The Lord's Prayer[1]

It happens every day. Debra, a junior at a prestigious Ivy League university, needs better grades. She downloads and submits someone else's research. Frank, a respected businessman, plugs a pen drive into his work laptop. Within seconds he's viewing inappropriate material and downloading copyrighted movies. April and Sara, two twelve-year-old girls from Kansas are pretending to be twenty-something "valley girls." They think they are chatting with the interesting nineteen-year-old hunk from Oregon in the picture. In reality, their online friend is a forty-three-year-old man who lives nearby. Abigail, a lonely mom, desperately misses her traveling husband. After stumbling across an old boyfriend online, her catching-up has become frequent flirting.

What do all of these people have in common? Each started in one part of cyberspace and ended up in another. Their online activities began with good intentions, but somehow things went astray. All of them underestimate their predicament. One by one, each will face serious consequences.

Scenes like these are repeated millions of times each day around the world. How did they get to that point? What are the long-term impacts? Are you next?

The Internet as we know it is less than twenty years old—barely out of its adolescence. But it already blankets the globe. The United States currently has over 215 million Internet users. Around the world, hundreds of millions of others connect to the Internet via a wide variety of wireless devices. China will soon have more Web surfers than the United States—mostly connecting via cell phone.[2] From e-banking to checking the news to chatting with friends, we now surf the Net as a business and personal imperative that seems to demand our attention on a 7 x 24 x 365 basis. More and more of our schools, hospitals, governments, and homes rely on the Internet for conducting business, gathering data, and improving efficiency. Technology skills are vitally important to our economy and everyone's future, with more that 85 percent of twenty-first-century jobs requiring computer literacy.[3] Ours is an always-connected, "e-everything" world.

Your Online Experience—No Accident

As we surf the Web, the ramification of clicking on various links may seem slight. Nevertheless, professional webpage designers have spent untold hours trying to manage your experience. Where are your eyes drawn? Why are you attracted to certain pictures or coaxed into taking a detour to see websites that you never intended to visit five minutes earlier? What makes you come back?

Selling various messages through TV, movies, newspapers, and other media has been going on for decades. Now the battle for your attention has moved into cyberspace. Since the mid-1990s, webpage designers have been working to perfect new techniques to attract and keep the interest of surfers. The concept of "tempting the click" was articulated over a decade ago:

> Tempting the click means replacing the "one-to-many" flow of conventional advertising communications with a "one-to-one" relationship that tunes the message to each prospect. . . . Keeping

the prospects coming back for more requires some special talents, as well. The best interactive art director might be working today as a video game designer, someone who knows how to keep a viewer nailed to his computer for hours, doling out just enough pleasure and just enough pain and turning a few seconds of attention into an on-line commitment.[4]

It may come as no surprise that advertising now works this way, but these techniques are being effectively used for negative purposes as well as for good. In fact, those who would do us harm are at the leading edge of tempting the click. Everyone understands that poll results can change dramatically by just changing a few words in a survey question, but do we understand how subtle changes on the Web can alter our behavior?

We can't go very far on the World Wide Web without experiencing powerful challenges to our values and beliefs. Just like virtual journeys in the movie *The Matrix*, visits into cyberspace can quickly become risky ventures. Exact numbers are impossible to verify, but attacks on integrity are occurring millions of times every day across America and around the world. Just as our global financial system is starting to come to grips with the immensity of the identity theft problem and devise some workable solutions, along comes his slicker, covert brother—integrity theft.

Put simply, we are participating in an extraordinary cyber battle over ethics and values. Your trustworthiness, character, and even religious beliefs are ultimately at stake. Regardless of the relative ease of clicking on a link, your online actions are affecting every area of your life.

David versus Goliath

Why do so many people suffer damage to their integrity online? One reason is that those who want to do the right things vastly underestimate the power and the sophistication of those who might tempt them toward less-than-virtuous pursuits on the Web. Put simply, the average Web surfer is outspent and outmaneuvered when it comes to temptations in cyberspace. Minimally, tens of billions of dollars are spent in Internet marketing each year, and well over $150 billion is spent on TV advertising.[5] While there is nothing wrong with advertising in and of itself, a large number of those ads try to tempt people into sin, to surf against their own values.

Let me be clear: we're dealing with a David-versus-Goliath situation—and you are David. The reality is that people slip by not understanding the scope of the problem, or the moral and spiritual risks they face. Millions think they are currently getting away with online shenanigans, but they're fooling only themselves.

Of course, for every answer to the perils of integrity theft, there are five more questions. Where's the line? Who decides what is bad? Is this a moral crusade? Once we decide what's what, we turn on filters. Yet it's easier for many kids, not to mention adults, to go around the filters than it was for Luke Skywalker to get around the storm troopers in *Star Wars*. Even when filtering software is working on one network, the functionality is generally not portable. In other words, those same websites aren't blocked as we access content at home, work, hotels, and libraries, via cell phones and other computers.

As a society, we focus attention on training children but pay little attention to the rest of us. Why do most stop caring about adult surfing habits, unless the behavior is illegal, when a person turns eighteen? There are various programs to help people after they've become addicted to activities such as viewing porn, or even addicted to online games, but little ethical guidance to prevent those addictions. Every parent knows that children, and especially teenagers, want to do whatever the adults are doing—not what they say. It gets very frustrating, so we are prone to give up trying.

This book will tackle some of these tough questions, but it all starts with an individual resolution. We must first understand the challenges and recognize the fight in front of us. The real issue is not blocking content, but "doing what you say and saying what you do." This book is about personal online integrity—and learning to recognize and repel the many, many challenges to integrity faced by anyone who goes online.

Another Battle?—I'll Pass . . .

If you're at all like me, another battle is not what you want or need right now. It seems as if there is never enough time in the day for a father with four active children and a busy wife who homeschools and leads children's programs at church. Most of us want out of the seemingly never-ending struggles around the world. Yet, truth be told, we are still drawn into pursuing various interests on the Web. Even with full schedules, we find time to check out politics, weather, sports, business news, entertainment, or other websites.

Like it or not, we're in this struggle for the rest of our lives. The importance of cyberspace will only grow as we move deeper into the twenty-first century. No matter what your reason for visiting a website or viewing an e-mail, once you click, the people who built the content control what you see. Many of us connect when we're tired and our "moral guards" are down. Increasingly, the advertisers are demanding their time. This can even mean taking over the entire screen for a few seconds to get their message across. Sure, that turns some people off, so their challenge is to make that commercial message just short enough that you won't click on the little *x* at the corner of the screen. If the user tries to scroll down or get rid of an annoying advertisement, the unwanted images will often follow.

Internet advertising that conflicts with your values is just a part of the problem. Another, larger, issue is even harder to fix. The culture of the Internet is developing in some very unhealthy ways. As later chapters describe in detail, online norms now encourage lying, cheating, stealing, and many varieties of cyber lust. These online behaviors have become so commonplace that they are even expected behaviors for many surfers. As any experienced sociologist (or chief information security officer) will tell you, changing entrenched culture is probably our biggest challenge.

Defining Integrity Theft

In its simplest form, integrity theft is the repeated attraction of others to do wrong. Usually caused by deliberate action, integrity theft harms others by tempting, luring, persuading, encouraging, or provoking the "target" to act in a manner that violates his or her true values, ethics, beliefs, or commitments. I use this figure of speech to highlight the reality that "small trespasses" can have significant and destructive impacts.

Integrity theft thrives in an online environment where almost anything goes. Many behaviors are encouraged in cyberspace that are considered taboo in the physical world. Millions of users make bad decisions, like posting inappropriate pictures or information on their MySpace pages, without realizing that their next job or acceptance into graduate school may be threatened.

Thinking that everyone is doing it, surfers also conveniently rename immoral activities. Plagiarism becomes copying text, stealing becomes downloading files, lying becomes protecting yourself—often without a second thought. Others think they are immune from consequences by hiding behind an anonymous screen name. These behaviors are growing exponentially in cyberspace.

Of course, as is the case with identity theft, integrity theft can happen without the Internet. The moral issues are not new. Temptations have existed since Adam and Eve ate the fruit. The twenty-first-century difference is the breadth and depth of the opportunities to do wrong online. Under the banner of "privacy protections," many engage in Web activities with a false name, which magnifies the appeal of cyber temptations and lowers normal "real-life" inhibitions.

I believe the impact of integrity theft is worse than that of identity theft, since it affects far more people every day. Also, succumbing to Internet temptations can lead to a loss of your reputation, job, or important relationships. These are much harder to fix than your credit history.

Some Quick Searches

Sports scores, term papers, shopping sprees, vacation deals, and history research are just a few of the millions of reasons people surf the Net each day. Powerful search engines like Google, Yahoo, Live, and

Ask can answer complicated questions and take us right where we want to be online. But very often we get unwanted material as well.

To get an immediate and vivid sense of the range of online temptations, try this experiment. Do Google searches on such innocuous terms as "mature" or "college girls." Table 1 lists the results of a few searches I recently conducted.

Google Key Phrase	Number of Results	Threats	Sample Temptation
"Fooling people"	Over 6.7 million	Lying, deception	Confessions of e-tricks, "E-mail greeting card hides porn."[6]
"Quick diploma"	Over 600,000	Cheating at school, fake degrees	Diploma in 5 days, Cheating students, "Poor Grades Aside, Athletes Get into College on a $399 Diploma."[7]
"Steal on Internet"	Over 1.3 million	Easy money, quick buck, Internet piracy	Online Job Scammers Steal Millions, Steal Neighbor's Internet, "How to Steal Wi-Fi."[8]
"College girl," "Women," or "Mature"	Over a billion	Lust, adultery, sex	Focus on porn, XXX, millions of pages of seductive material, dating while married, Girls Gone Wild, Sex Hungry Moms

Table 1. Dotcom Temptations Are Threats to Your Integrity[9]

But even if you are surprised by the breadth and depth of e-temptations, you may be wondering: "Can't you just filter out this porn and other stuff with a software package loaded onto your PC?" Not very easily. I performed the searches in table 1 after activating one of the most powerful third-party content filters on the market. If you click on one of these linked sites, most filtering programs will block some of the content, but many parents (and other users) are not aware that searches themselves are not filtered.

The simple truth is that the vast majority of families and businesses do not filter these links when searching. They are a huge and powerful temptation made available under the guise of assisting our search with "related content." However, these links are intentionally placed where they are to lure millions into going where others want you to go. If the companies that make search engines wanted to "clean up" access to these sites, they could simply change the way software initially works, resetting the "default filter."

But companies claim that they offer what people want to see. They also state that we viewers have the technical ability to stop seeing whatever we deem inappropriate material. Still, most people either don't know how, or never bother to try, to change default settings. Yes, some people are intentionally searching for this content, but many others end up in a far different place than intended when they connect. Web designers know this, and the advertisers take advantage of this fact to make money.

What about online sites other than search engines? I visit a popular weather site. While I check out the local forecast, an enticing box pops up, with a beautiful young woman depicted wearing lingerie, and not much of it. I'm invited to see this advertiser's summer 25-percent-off sale and more "baby dolls." By design, these large advertisements are seldom blocked by your family-friendly filter. The picture grows to instantly take over the entire screen before settling back into a box that is larger than the weather map. Do I click on that flashing picture with the pretty smile? Scenes like this are repeated thousands of times a day across the world.

While it is easy to criticize companies like Google or Microsoft, it is important to understand that the services they offer are "free" to us because advertisers pay for the space. In economic terms, there is nothing wrong with this model. The problem comes when, in virtual reality, the surfer's values are routinely violated or eroded. The definition of what is publicly acceptable seems constantly to grow broader, or more degraded. We need new "win-win" approaches that don't repeatedly violate the moral and ethical boundaries of so many of us who use the Internet daily.

Assessing Virtual Values by Examining Current Choices

Internet companies want to get to know us better and develop personalized relationships with customers that enable them to answer questions more accurately. Their goal is better-targeted marketing. They want to provide results that are simpler to use—not thousands or millions of irrelevant results. If they are to do that, they'll need to get to know our values as well. In fact, we want those values built into our surfing experience.

In the simplest terms, to surf your values means to match your online life with your offline values and beliefs. It means saying what you will do before you go online, and doing what you've said once you're connected. There are a variety of technology tools and preference settings that are currently available to help people maintain their integrity.

Historically, the main way that most families and workplaces have expressed their desire to maintain their values while on the Internet has been through filtering out whatever is deemed as the "bad stuff." But as we will discuss in the next chapter, this defensive strategy lacks breadth and depth—mainly because unwanted content gets past the filters, and helpful content is sometimes blocked. In addition, we need to encourage the good we want to do and not just focus on eliminating the bad. As any good football coach will tell you, the best defense is a good offense, and blocking content (alone) is not a good offense—not a positive long-term answer.

Although limited in scope, the Internet still offers us a variety of ways to surf our values today. These choices are revealed by the websites we visit, what we do when we get to those sites, the people we interact with, and even the amount of time we spend instant-messaging others. What favorite websites have you bookmarked or made quickly accessible on your computer? What features are you looking for? Once you get there, do you tell the truth about your age or circumstances?

The relationships we value most can also be seen by the shortcuts we create on our cell phones. We establish communities on Facebook and MySpace that allow only trusted friends to participate. Some even express their values by joining "Christian alternative" Web portals such as GodTube.com instead of YouTube.com.

Personalizing Choices

Another way that our values are currently expressed is through personalization. Visiting Google.com, you may choose the "SafeSearch" feature under preferences and apply "strict filtering" or "no filtering."

Strict filtering can dramatically reduce the amount of explicit content exposed in searches. When creating personal MySpace or Facebook pages, we are presented with a wide variety of settings. These can either limit access to our content or make content widely available. Once we make our choices, we are often encouraged by peer pressure, or even by the service itself, to choose a less restrictive preference. As a member of LinkedIn,[10] I am often urged to open up my profile to a wider audience, with the benefits portrayed in terms of more career opportunities or more professional contacts.

Most families also purchase security or privacy products from their internet service provider (ISP) or companies like Symantec or McAfee. These products and services will help stop unwanted porn and spam, and provide extra protection from security risks like viruses and scams. They offer an ever-increasing number of ways to detect fraud and even the likelihood of identity theft. Wouldn't it be nice if products could similarly monitor actions to detect integrity theft? Think of something like the sagacious and beneficial wizards that pop up to help in Microsoft Word, only these wizards would help us maintain our values.

Experts predict that we will soon be able to benefit from sophisticated personalized agents that will help us sift through Internet information for the digital content that we are looking for.[11] The computer security industry has caught on to the idea that security and privacy functionality should be built into the product from the start. For example, getting security and other updates from Microsoft can now happen automatically, whereas updates were previously awkward to apply. The concept of "secure by default" is catching on, but we're a long way from achieving the desired result. So, as an initial step, I urge you to check the default setting on new software as you install it on computers. Such attention at installation will later help you opt in to the right preferences.

Background Learning and Cookies

Do you ever wonder how Amazon.com knows what books you might want to buy? They keep track of what items you have looked at and what you bought, to make suggestions. They even take this information and send you e-mails regarding upcoming deals, free shipping promotions, and other changes that may interest you. Websites like Amazon keep track of your preferences with "persistent cookies," small files on your computer that track your online behaviors. When you come back, they recognize you and personalize your shopping. I enjoy this convenience, since Amazon has reminded me of what I was previously doing, after many an interruption.

Google and other search companies use cookies to keep a profile of your search habits. Their goal is to understand your interests and make results more relevant.

> As it works right now, if you use a Google product (Gmail, Google toolbar, AdWords, etc.), Google is keeping track of what you search for and what websites you visit, and it's then tailoring your results appropriately. Search for "bass," and Google will know whether you mean the fish or the instrument. . . . Seems it won't be long before Google knows what you're searching for before you do.[12]

Of course, you can turn off cookies in your browser so that companies can't track you, because many people feel uncomfortable with this level of tracking. Nevertheless, if you don't opt out or opt in somehow when you go online, you will get the default experience of that website.

Get ready for the Amazon experience to become the norm online. Everyone wants to get to know us and build an ongoing relationship. Whether they sell flowers or sports equipment, online retailers want us to be repeat customers. Ease of use is essential, and the better they can "get in our head," the more likely we'll be coming back the next time.

Opt In to Integrity

Almost every destination in cyberspace presents us with options that will affect our integrity in some way. Unfortunately, these options are often mislabeled as either "adult" or "child," rather than "moral" or "immoral." It often takes an extra effort to do the right thing. Many websites and games claim to offer "family-friendly" versions of their products, but the default settings are very different straight out of the box. Christians need to take the time to opt in to the available preference that best matches their values. More on this in later chapters.

Opting in to a values-based experience on the Internet won't stop others from going to sites that they value, but it will provide support for those who desire to live out their faith. I made wedding vows to be true to my wife, Priscilla, "until death do us part." I also said, "Forsaking all others, I will love and protect her." I wasn't forced to say those words. I hope, and even expect, that anyone and everyone that has my best interests at heart will support my vows. This includes not only friends and family, but my employer and companies that want my business. Hundreds of millions of people in this world have made similar wedding vows. They should expect no less.

One quick, yet probing, question I often ask myself to test whether I'm acting with integrity is this: "Am I being a hypocrite by clicking?" In his famous "Seven Woes" sermon found in Matthew 23, Jesus condemns the teachers of the law and Pharisees as hypocrites because, despite the fact that they knew what was right and wrong, their actions didn't match their words. We need to ask ourselves if we are acting with integrity or being hypocritical in our online conduct. Self-examination is another important first step.

We are all susceptible to online integrity theft, but in response you can start to change your behaviors right now. I'm also optimistic that new coalitions can be forged to transform the Internet culture into allowing an "opt-in," values-based Web surfing. Consider the parallel of cultural changes in cigarette smoking. Societal views on smoking cigarettes changed dramatically, once the risks were widely publicized. Smoking is still legal, as I believe it should be. But just as more smoke-free environments are available each day, new options to traverse the Internet without leaving behind our values and virtue are possible as well.

Nothing less than our families, businesses, and personal integrity is at stake in this battle. As with cigarettes, will it take another century to get this right? Most important, how can we please God as we integrate the Internet into more areas of life? How can we enjoy cyberspace, benefit from distance learning, communicate more conveniently and effectively, and yet truly preserve our integrity online? Let's start connecting the dots.

2 ➡ Why Filtering Is Not Enough

Problems with Parental Controls

We can't solve problems by using the same kind of thinking we used when we created them.

Albert Einstein[1]

When I discuss online temptations with someone for the first time, I typically get responses that fit into one of two categories. Most often I hear a candid response like, "My family is all set. We just block bad stuff with 'xyz' software package." Or sometimes I hear, "No problem. We just rely on our Internet service providers to take care of it." Those proud, but naive, comments represent a fairly typical attitude, even among Christians. Immediately, a red flag goes up in my mind.

Sometimes, I run into another group of people who are fairly open about their need for help. They seek out "computer geeks" like me to come over and load software to stop spam and viruses or get out of a technical bind. Many try their best to read the manual and follow procedures, but even with the best of intentions, they can never seem to keep their PCs out of trouble or their eyes from going astray.

Whether you have in-depth technical knowledge or run for computer help, you face different aspects of the same problem. Just as going to H&R Block doesn't relieve you of your responsibility to give honest answers to tax questions, relying on someone else for computer help doesn't lessen the need for accountability and integrity when surfing the Internet.

Why Filtering Alone Won't Work

Before I get into the limitations of filtering software, I want to make it clear that there are many excellent companies in the content filtering business. Most of them provide an important service that offers an essential component in assisting families and businesses in safely using the Internet. Companies like Symantec, Websense, McAfee, and Microsoft are on the front lines of addressing the never-ending security and privacy challenges on the Internet. There are many "how to" websites and articles on the importance of blocking porn, spyware, worms, viruses, and a myriad of other bad things, so I won't dwell on this topic.[2]

Many ISPs and cable companies also bundle filtering solutions into their monthly charges. Google, Live, Yahoo, and Ask even have manually controlled filtering levels for performing searches.

In addition, there are many smaller filtering and security companies that add important functionality, such as accountability software—which I discuss in later chapters. For more information on picking the best filtering product for your family, I recommend visiting an independent website that compares various products in multiple categories, such as Filter Review.[3] This website also provides contact information for organizations that protect children and families from pornography and age-inappropriate material.

Now the bad news. None of these companies can even come close to providing a complete solution to the integrity-theft problem. In fact, advertisements proclaiming complete "child-safe" or "family-friendly" solutions are part of the confusion. For example, in January 2007 our house was sent a pretty color flyer from a large cable company trying to sell us high-speed Internet service. The two bold words on the front were "Surf" and "Safe." The flyer opened up to describe their new offer. Was this false advertising? I'm not a lawyer, so I can't say. Perhaps their solution keeps you safe from computer viruses, but it certainly can't protect you morally.

My point is that technology solutions are only one part of any healthy Internet diet. Filtered Internet, which is sometimes called Internet parental controls, often increases misunderstandings by providing a false sense of security. Like shoppers browsing shelves in supermarkets being drawn to junk food, naive surfers can think anything that "gets through the filter" must be okay. In addition, it is not difficult to bypass filters, surf anonymously, move to other computers or networks without filters, or just turn the filters off.

Table 2 summarizes the limitations to current approaches. The biggest mistake has been to oversell the current level of protection. The truth is that this problem starts at an individual level and requires much more than just loading a software package onto your PC or paying your ISP an extra $5 or $10 a month for a filtered solution—even though filters can help, especially with kids.

Too often, technology products are presented as magic bullets that are as simple to use as smoke detectors, requiring only the equivalent of an annual battery change. Promises are often over-blown and expectations are rarely met, even when you follow all the instructions. An important point to consider is that the Internet is changing very rapidly. The focus of most filtering and security products is to block yesterday's problems. But once one technical problem is solved, another soon develops.

Every good project manager realizes that successful problem solving requires change in three core areas: people, processes, and technology. To a large extent, technology is the easiest part and takes the least amount of effort. Yes, researching and installing the right product is very important. But just as we buy a software package to help with tax preparation, loading software is only the beginning of the integrity-protection process. And unlike taxes, our Web surfing is not a once-a-year activity.

Common Perception (or Advertised As)	Technical Reality
Easy to use	Easy to install. Hard to maintain. Requires frequent upgrades. Often confused with security and various other PC bundles.
Comprehensive	Usually based on URL (link name). Focus is on children. Does not cover subtle temptations. Most categories never configured. Hard to control consistently. Not portable to phones, a BlackBerry, or other devices.
Runs by itself	Requires care and feeding. Exceptions need handholding. Other software interferes, disables, or overwrites controls (e.g.: spyware removal software). ISP makes decisions for you.
Built in to free or public wireless Internet access	Many "hotspots" are unfiltered. Criminals even use lack of controls to hide activities.
Secure	Administrators, often Mom or Dad, are exempt or bypass filters. Children get passwords or find ways to surf around filters.

Table 2. Web Filtering Packages and ISP Solutions

People Issues—From Vision to Action

What are the "people issues"? I'll introduce this topic now and cover it in more detail in later chapters. People issues include creating a vision of what individuals and families want and don't want to see (based upon values), training users, placing PCs in common areas, rewarding people for proper behavior, disciplining inappropriate behavior, developing good online habits, and so on. I challenge individuals to decide if they want to "opt in" to virtuous surfing with some type of an online commitment (or cyber pledge) of integrity. No software package or ISP can do that for you.

Why is a proactive opting-in so vital? Self-proclaimed "Internet freedom fighters" are battling to enable "circumvention technologies" or allow content to go around filters via a variety of sophisticated means.[4] There are many people and organizations, such as the Electronic Frontier Foundation (EFF), that support TOR, a tool to surf anonymously. "Individuals use TOR to keep websites from tracking them and their family members, or to connect to news sites, instant messaging services, or the like when these are blocked by their local Internet providers."[5]

What's more disturbing is the number of articles published not only by hackers, but by prestigious media like the *Wall Street Journal Online*, that describe in detail how to circumvent security and filtering controls that are put in place.[6] My point is that there are ways to get around protections if they are viewed as barriers, and many sites online are willing to help you do it.

Some Internet content companies even sell a "link of the day" to get to normally filtered content, such as porn at work. What is going on is a kind of "mini-arms race" between the content pushers and the content blockers. This behind-the-scenes cyber battle is actually growing more intense and won't end anytime soon. (The same is true of companies sending spam e-mails and those who are trying to block spam.)

In 2007, the State of Michigan government sites received around 255 million e-mails via the Internet. Over 225 million were either spam or viruses and were turned back by our security measures. Still, many thousands of e-mails that lure people down the "primrose path" got through. While those technical details go beyond the scope of this book, it is clear that the motive of Internet users regarding e-temptation is paramount.

Other users turn to wireless "hotspots" to gain portable, unfiltered access to the Internet. Simply by using their wireless card, which is pre-installed on most computers, people can surf on many networks anonymously and filter-free. Since people are now so mobile and regularly moving between thousands of Internet access points, many experts argue that placing filters on laptops and "endpoint" devices such as phones is a better solution than relying on filtered Internet from ISPs. I recommend both protections. But either way, personal intentions and habits are vital.

Consider this example from the summer of 2006:

Detectives went to an apartment building in Arlington County, VA, warrant in hand, to nab a suspected pedophile who had traded child pornography online. It was to be a routine, mostly effortless arrest. But when they pounded on the door, detectives found an elderly woman who, they quickly concluded, had nothing to do with the crime. The real problem was her computer's wireless router, a device sending a signal through her 10-story building and allowing savvy neighbors a free path to the Internet from the privacy of their homes.[7]

Process Issues—Keep It Going

Addressing Internet "process issues" ensures that everyone understands the rules and follows them on an ongoing basis. In simple terms, we need a repeatable checklist that works. We all need to be accountable for our actions, and we'll later cover this in detail. Communication between parents and children, husband and wife, or employees and human resources is vital to maintain transparency and accountability. Many individuals, families, or businesses start out very well on the cyber journey, setting up excellent protections. However, over time, they get too busy, overwhelmed, or disinterested to continue the fight.

Unfortunately, these process activities often get piled into a seemingly never-ending list of "family PC issues," like virus protection, spyware removal, backing up hard drives, updating the operating system, loading new games and software, fixing problems with a technical-support helpdesk that is slow to answer the phone, and so forth. It's fairly common to have one person in every house who is in charge of all of these duties, but who's watching that person? Many individuals just give up and go online to surf even when protections aren't working properly. Like a five-year-old running across a four-lane interstate highway, they may not realize the danger until it's too late.

In the workplace, most companies have their own filters in place, but they vary widely in their scope and effectiveness. In fact, many Christians have stricter filters at home than at work. However, in order to follow company policies, most people cannot load their home filtering software on their work desktop or laptop computers. When you add in the faster connectivity that usually exists at work, and the amount of time that people sit in front of a PC, the temptations to surf inappropriately are often greater at work than at home.

It's also important to note that thousands of people every day suffer integrity theft online without any overt content-blocking issues. Activities such as sending flirtatious e-mails to a colleague at work, chatting on a date site, or watching suggestive videos on YouTube.com are typically not blocked. Still, I have seen those simple activities eventually lead to marriage breakups or respected people resigning or being removed from their jobs. I repeat: no technology alone will ever solve this problem! This is more like a marathon than a sprint, so we need repeatable processes.

The "Biggest" Problem

Even when everyone in your family or business agrees on what's needed, when your software is working correctly, and when the right ongoing processes are in place, temptations still pour in. Why? Current filtering products, and more importantly the websites we visit, are not built around our values. Yes, filters can easily block certain websites, like Playboy.com, or even categories within wider websites, like ladies' intimate apparel. However, as discussed briefly in chapter 1, they don't block embedded temptations within the websites or new types of advertisements that come with the content or service.

While some filters can block all pop-up content or advertisements, these features are often not used or are too broad to be an effective long-term solution that creates a win-win for the advertisers who pay for the free content and those who view it. Believe it or not, companies now hire professional surfers to gauge whether their messages are getting through and to post positive company reviews on blogs.[8] It is important to remember that as the Internet moves forward, the companies paying for websites will expand their demands that their advertisements are seen as more services are offered.

A more subtle problem is the tempting content that shows up only occasionally. We visit a certain website and have no moral issue with the content nine times out of ten. However, on the tenth occasion, BAM! We are lured into an intriguing temptation that leads us to lie, cheat, or steal. In addition, the content on many sites is specifically built to not trigger the filtering software most people are running. Like a fish that sees the bait floating in the water, but not the hook, you may be lured into Web content—often in violation of your values. This is done by design. Many Web developers see e-temptation as an art form or acquired skill that requires knowing what is and is not typically blocked via filters.

Everyone surfs in unique ways, so you may wonder how we can possibly solve this problem and personalize online experiences for different people. Men and women are tempted by different things. When we start to categorize who is tempted by what, it can get complicated with married, single, young, old, and so on. How can we segment audiences? What about personal preferences? I'll grapple with these issues in more depth, but first we need to consider another element in order to see the big picture of threats to online integrity that are only now emerging.

What about Parental TV Controls?

People have been fighting for decency regulations on television for years. Sex, violence, and physical abuse, not to mention lying, cheating, and stealing, are glorified at all hours of the day on TV. The cable and satellite networks use free-speech protections to claim exemptions from the rules governing the likes of ABC, NBC, and CBS. They claim that they are giving viewers what they want to see and that they are customer-focused. Many cable station websites link to a message like this:

> The cable industry has a longstanding commitment to addressing parents' concerns about what they and their children see on television. . . . Cable's approach to addressing indecency and violence on television is based on the concepts of Control, Choice and Education.[9]

There are many books and websites that can help implement parental controls. New TV sets must have a "V-chip"[10] installed, which assists in blocking TV programs. The TV Boss.org[11] provides information on a variety of parental options for controlling your TV. Focus on the Family also provides many helpful articles and guides at their Plugged In Online website.[12]

Although sometimes helpful, current TV controls are fundamentally flawed for several reasons. First and foremost, the focus is only on children and not on millions of morality-minded adults. Even the names "parental controls" and "adult entertainment" show the limitations of current approaches. As every marketing company knows, names are very important. We need a model that includes everyone who, like Job, says, "I made a covenant with my eyes."[13] Why not start by renaming the entire concept to "integrity" or even "my family values" controls?

Second, advanced parental controls are not available to some customers. You need to have the right TV with chip, set-top box, and/or software. The focus of advertising for cable and satellite TV is to get customers to subscribe to more channels and pay more each month. Filters are generally treated as a feature that the majority of customers don't use. Networks rely on people to change the channel or turn off material that is thought to be offensive.

Third, parental controls are hard to use, and few people even know about, much less follow, parental controls that they can use. Some parents know even less about how to use these controls than their older children do. As in Web filtering, even when everything is working properly, the older children and adults have the passwords and bypasses to allow them to do whatever they like. Often, temptations become too great when other family members are away from home.

While most parents take steps to monitor what their children are watching, few use the current available technology. In a 2006 poll, Russell Research uncovered the following statistics:

> The tools parents personally use range from watching TV with children (63%), limiting TV watching to certain shows (61%) and times (55%); using TV ratings (52%), using cable controls (17%), satellite controls (12%) or the v-chip (5%).[14]

We need a new model. People should be able to surf their values. New options need to be easy to use and comprehensive. Yes, it should be an "opt-in" solution, which will put many privacy advocates at ease. Options can be implemented without violating freedom-of-speech protections and forcing others to comply with one's values. I hope the cable and satellite stations are truly open to customer input for positive change to bring the industry in line with what families really want.

Double Trouble—Web and TV Merge

Why do I devote attention to television in a book about online integrity? Because technology has exploded in amazing ways in recent years. Back in the 1980s, few people predicted, or even dreamed about, the global Internet. As late as the mid-1990s, Bill Gates even underestimated the importance of the World Wide Web. Now we can watch TV on the Web, and we use the Net to answer survey questions from the shows we watch on TV. Our phones, TV, and Internet are merging into one. I tell my children that our society is heading toward the Dick Tracy watch with full-motion, two-way voice and video—priced similarly to current cell phones. The twenty-first century is surely bringing us exciting new toys. But a quick look at television trends reveals that with the good comes the bad.

Like millions of people, I enjoy watching the Super Bowl, the World Series, or a family-friendly movie. Unfortunately, we can't watch any of these without cable and satellite commercials that tempt viewers with R-rated bedroom scenes from upcoming movies and TV programs. One Saturday in July, I was watching Major League Baseball with my four-year-old son, Paul, when *Sex and the City* commercials appeared. Today, your only option is to change the channel or turn off the TV. While new technology allows program recordings and eliminating commercials, the same ads are showing up in new ways—like during ballgames in a corner of the TV screen or even at popular online websites like MySpace.com.

These advertisers are not respecting our personal or family values. I call what they're doing "virtual trespassing." Commercials come into our homes and try to seduce us into watching programs that I normally would never contemplate watching. Why call it "trespassing"? I would never allow that material or those messages into my house if given a choice. Remember, we're heading into a new world where virtual reality will blur the difference between our real and virtual worlds much further.

What behaviors are subtly sold? In February 2008, a commercial promoting *Paradise Hotel 2* ended with a woman looking into the camera and proudly saying, "Everyone lies in this place."[15] Similarly, in the United Kingdom, TV shows like *Hotel Babylon* glorify greed—with characters who work at a fictitious five-star London hotel doing just about anything to make more money.[16]

Beyond the irritations that you may feel, these messages increasingly, albeit gradually, challenge your beliefs and convictions. Over time, the radical and extreme become commonplace. Occasionally, the sponsors go too far and society reacts. A great example of this is the Janet Jackson Super Bowl performance in 2005. The "wardrobe malfunction" led to numerous complaints and new standards for broadcasters—who quickly apologized. No matter where you go in the virtual world to get information or entertainment, there is a subliminal battle occurring, whether you recognize it or not.

It's also important to understand that as more extreme websites, advertisements, TV shows, and movies push the envelope and shrink the definition of "shocking," the mainline sites and shows feel the need to participate to keep market share. The ethical line between right and wrong is moving fast. We all need to discuss appropriate lines that we won't cross with family members.

Cell Phones and BlackBerries

It was a cold Michigan Saturday in January 2007, and my fourteen-year-old daughter, Katherine, and I headed to the Sprint store to buy her a new cell phone. She was delighted to pick out the light pink "Katana" model from Sanyo. We purchased a plan where she shared minutes with her mom, who also got a new phone. This was a big decision for her, since the monthly charges were going to eat up most of her allowance. Still, she wanted to take the plunge, as her friends had done. Katherine would spend the next few days playing with the dozens of features, ringtones, and screen savers. I had no idea how big a deal this was for her and other teenagers.

As we checked out, I was informed that thirty days of free mobile Web access was mandatory on all new phones, but I could cancel that service twenty-four hours later if I called back. We couldn't afford this $40 a month feature, so I fully intended to disable Internet access the next day.

The next morning, I got to thinking about the fact that millions of people access the Web via cell phones, and I wondered if they had filtered Internet as a default setting. I spent over an hour reading through the manual but couldn't find anything about enabling or disabling Web filters or any ways to block content. I did learn about features named "cellflirt" and "webdate" that made me somewhat uncomfortable. I also noticed that "girls" was the top search the week before. As it turned out, no filtering was available at that time.

Many parents buy their children cell phones not knowing or thinking about the Web browser embedded within the phone—until they get the bill. What happens in the meantime? Where are children (and adults) tempted to surf with their cell phones? (As we mentioned earlier, cell phones are the primary Internet access device in many countries, such as China.)

What about BlackBerries or work-issued devices with Web access? Most of those devices don't go through company Web filtering software. In a very ironic coincidence, I got to work on the following Monday morning, only to be briefed by the State of Michigan's senior cyber risk manager on a new problem. A few staff were caught using their Sprint PCS (wireless Internet) cards to bypass work Web filters. We also discussed unfiltered wireless "hotspots" that were being accessed at local restaurants. Such temptations are real, are growing more popular, and are difficult to fix.

Censorship versus Real Choices

For so many reasons, then, we need new options with real choices. The advertisers don't win when people turn off their TVs or block all the advertisements online, so why not tailor content to audiences? We have the technology available today to offer desired alternatives. I challenge the content providers, television networks, and advertisers to step up and offer real alternatives to stop this race to the bottom in tempting programming that steals integrity and can destroy reputations and families.

Don't people have the right to watch what they want and go wherever they'd like in cyberspace? Sure, but they shouldn't be able to force others to listen to or view content that violates their religious or moral values—which is the current norm.

When I go to a popular steak restaurant, I'm not forced to eat seafood. Imagine this scene:

Waiter Phil: "Welcome to Bob's steakhouse. My name is Phil, and I'm here to serve you."

Dan: "Thanks, it's great to be here. I'm ready for a nice juicy steak."

Phil: "Can I get you a large plateful of seafood to start you off?"

Dan: "No, just the steak special please, and some ice water with lemon."

Phil: "If you won't eat a large plateful of seafood first, you'll need to leave! It's our rule."

Dan: "What? This is a steakhouse. I'm allergic to seafood. You can't make me eat seafood. I'm willing to have a Diet Coke with my meal, but I don't like, nor can I eat, seafood."

Phil: "I'm sorry, sir. Those are the rules. We can't serve you."

This restaurant scene is absurd at one level, but it represents the norm in our current media world. My daughter loves *American Idol*, but we sometimes feel the need to turn off the TV during the commercials. Why not allow personalized or family-based alternatives during popular programs?

Some may wonder how these examples are any different from other advertisements that you may not want to see. Perhaps you like bottled water and not Coke, and you'd rather not see a Coke commercial for health reasons. The difference is in ethical or moral behavior and what has traditionally been called "tempting into sin." Still, there is no reason why "surfing your values" couldn't, *from a technological perspective*, someday include foods that tempt you. As discussed in the introduction, honesty and integrity are important values to the vast majority in society, but few would view drinking a Coke as an ethical violation. These cyber temptations are still threatening to your family, your job, and your values.

So who's in control? Are we driving change, or is change driving us? The answer is both. New technology is enabling new interactive possibilities and the personal involvement of millions of people who offer pictures, blogs, video clips, and more at global social networking sites, but even experts don't really know where this will take us in a decade. Bill Gates, in early 1993, said, "The Internet? We're not interested in it." In 2007 he said the Internet is set to revolutionize television within five years, due to an explosion of online video content and the merging of PCs and TV sets.[17]

I want to assure you that I'm NOT advocating a hide-in-the-hills or throw-away-your-computer approach to the future. I'm a pro-Internet, eBay-using, Web-surfing family guy—yes, you might even say a "cyber geek." (Since my bachelor's and master's degrees are in computer science, I automatically qualify.) I'm an optimist about the future, but we need to make a few sharp turns to get there.

In the next few chapters I will show the implications of going down these dangerous roads with the belief that your life won't be impacted or your relationships put in jeopardy. There is no doubt that any new model needs to be flexible, based upon a wide variety of factors.

3 ➡ Who's Fooling Whom in Cyberspace?

Overcoming Online Deception

All mortals tend to turn into the thing they are pretending to be.

C. S. Lewis[1]

In November 2005, an eighteen-year old high school senior named Michael Sessions entered the national spotlight when he was elected mayor of Hillsdale, Michigan.[2] Running as a write-in candidate for the town of 8,200, he won by just two votes. Sessions became an instant hero. Young Christians held him and his campaign manager up as the model for involvement.

Michael isn't the only young adult who deserves The Rebelution's[3] attention. On the night of the swearing-in ceremony, Brandon Thomas, the mayor's 17-year-old campaign manager, demonstrated a knack for good politics as he explained a downtown clean-up campaign he and Michael organized on Sunday.[4]

Hillsdale became a media hotspot.

> [Sessions's] swearing-in brought more than 20 camera crews from
> as far away as Japan and Russia. A March 2007 city council meeting
> brought a Shanghai TV crew. . . . "But it's OK," he said. "It's good for
> Hillsdale. And I like staying busy because it keeps you goal-oriented
> and . . . out of trouble." If it's not meeting with the governor or giving
> Rotary speeches, it's interviews with Montel or Letterman.[5]

And then, less than two years after the election, he was in the
headlines again, but this time only a plea bargain kept him out of
jail. On Independence Day 2007, the *Detroit News* ran this story,
"Hillsdale's Teen Mayor Convicted in Web Prank."[6] According to
the report,

> Sessions pleaded no contest to sending an e-mail under someone
> else's name to the mother of a former friend, accusing him of drink-
> ing and running around with women. In return for the plea, prosecu-
> tors dropped a more serious charge: that Sessions had hacked into
> the friend's MySpace and America Online accounts to delete his lists
> of personal contacts with their addresses and phone numbers.
>
> Sessions, who was convicted of malicious annoyance by writing,
> was ordered by a Hillsdale County district judge to perform 40 hours
> of community service and pay $850 in restitution and $100 in court
> costs.

Within days, everything changed for the teen idol. "Crime and
punishment easily enter discussions in Hillsdale, and there's plenty
of head shaking and eye rolling over the behavior of Mayor Michael
Sessions, accompanied by remarks like 'How could he be so stupid?'
Adding tension to the drama is an effort to oust Sessions through
a recall campaign."[7]

"It was done out of anger and frustration,"[8] Hillsdale county pros-
ecutor Neal Brady said. The young mayor made a public apology for
his mistakes. His reputation suffered, and he faced the consequences
for his actions. Many Hillsdale residents and outside observers now
write off the entire incident as an immature mistake made by a teenager. We all take wrong turns. Let's just forgive and forget.

Is there a moral to this story? I think so. No matter who you are or what you've accomplished in life, your cyber sins will eventually find you out. Just as shoplifters who aren't caught will typically proceed to steal more expensive items, most deceptive surfers foolishly graduate to bigger and more harmful cyber escapades. Their lies grow like Pinocchio's nose. Only facing the truth allows a new beginning.

While voluntary confession is always best, getting caught and facing the law can be a hidden blessing. There are thousands of online stories from those who thank God that they were caught in their cyber trespasses by a family member or coworker before the consequences of their actions became more severe and they faced jail time or worse.

While we'll never know what might have happened if Mayor Sessions had never been caught, what about the cyber behavior from millions of others? What lies are floating around your corner of cyberspace? More importantly, are you fooling others or currently being deceived online?

Deception on the Web

Americans love to search for information. Never before has so much data been so widely and easily available to the masses. No longer content to wait for tomorrow's newspaper or even the evening news, we now demand instant updates on events happening on the other side of the world. In this new Web 2.0 experience, we are also contributors via blogs, wiki updates, comments to articles, and personal Web pages that become news.

But can we trust what we see online? How many times have you thought, "That can't be right. Is that really true?" or "Did he/she really say that?"

Finding another opinion or checking the source is always a good idea. For example, a Google search conducted in September 2007 for the phrase "When did Columbus discover America?" yielded almost two million results. However, the top site insisted that Columbus discovered America in 1485 and not 1492.[9] The next website insisted that Columbus never really discovered America at all.[10] Good luck with your homework.

While cyberspace provides access to great sources of authoritative information, it is also a virtual dumping ground full of inaccurate quotes, partial truths, and deliberate lies. Most surfers know that the Internet is full of misinformation, hoaxes, scams, counterfeit websites, and opinions that are portrayed as facts. And yet we've become conditioned to rush to websites with sensational headlines, even if the underlying fact or principle is ridiculous.

Has popularity become truth? Consider this story from Reuters as an example of the widespread perception that a high number of Web visits can somehow make a thing true.

> A senior French politician, now a minister in President Nico-las Sarkozy's government, suggested last year that US President George W. Bush might have been behind the September 11, 2001 attacks. . . . Asked in an interview last November, before she became minister, whether she thought Bush might be behind the attacks, Christine Boutin says: "I think it is possible. I think it is possible. . . . I know that the websites that speak of this problem are websites that have the highest number of visits. . . . And I tell myself that this expression of the masses and of the people cannot be without truth."[11]

The Internet has taken the phrase "perception is reality" to a new level. Spam messages arrive from an expert insisting we have a once-in-a-lifetime opportunity to buy a stock. These "pump-and-dump" scams are notorious for temporarily increasing the value of a company. Thousands ignore reality and buy based on hearsay. Who cares what the stock is really worth, as long as you can get in and out before the price drops?

Spam e-mails promise cheap drugs or better mortgages, or they spread urban legends. Cleverly packaged messages take advantage of world events to fool the naive into responding. Often, friends forward myths from a seemingly trusted source promising money for forwarding the message further. You'd better check "urban legends" sites, such as www.snopes.com or www.truthminers.com, because these offers are usually too good to be true. While you're at it, be careful to check the blog you're reading. Some fake blogs (or "flogs") imitate expert sources, or websites fool readers by offering material under someone else's name.

For example, millions of electronic cards (e-cards) are sent from what appears to be a family member but really provide a link downloading viruses. Other scams imitate the police or the FBI to convince recipients that the e-mail is real.

> The U.S. FBI's Internet Crime Complaint Center (IC3) is warning of fraudulent e-mails that appear to come from the FBI and U.S. military. "The IC3 has increasingly received intelligence of fraudulent schemes misrepresenting the FBI and/or Director Robert S. Mueller III. The fraudulent e-mails give the appearance of legitimacy due to the usage of pictures of the FBI Director, seal, letter head, and/or banners."[12]

What's to be done? The Congress, state legislatures, and technology companies have been debating various technical and legal aspects of spam and related problems for the past decade, but the problems continue to worsen. Due to the significant money being made by sophisticated and organized cyber criminals, the spammers are winning, often by basing their operations overseas. Despite the fact that a few very large FBI busts have been made, laws regulating spam are largely ignored with minimal consequence. More on this topic in chapter 5.

Just Ignore It?

Knowing few scams are punished, our society has moved on and adapted to a cyber world full of urgent messages that are ignored. We've adjusted to the con artists by trashing emergency e-mails and ignoring supposedly critical instant messages. This new normal has created a dangerous backdrop for a postmodern culture that is again asking Pilate's question, "What is truth?" The unwritten moral code within cyberspace has become "whatever it takes to get attention."

In a world where a Boy Scout medal or a ten-year service award at work no longer suffices, a new battle to get noticed is occurring in written and video forms. This silent scream for significance plays out in home stunts and exaggerated advertising claims. For example, the "cool new videos" highlighted on the front page of MySpace on September 15, 2007, portrayed crazy pictures with the captions: "Car Lifted with Firehose" and "Laughing Yoga Exercise." Clicking on a flashing color link that boldly asked, "Want to know who has a crush on you?" yielded an advertisement with flirting tips, for $9.95 a month.[13] Other pages sell hints to increase your number of friends or "pimp" your site.

While cyberspace enables new innovative forms of communication, some experts mourn the latest advances. "Say good-bye to today's experts and cultural gatekeepers—our reporters, news anchors, editors, music companies, and Hollywood movie studios. In today's cult of the amateur, the monkeys are running the show."[14]

Many others say "good riddance" to Hollywood, but don't rule out big media yet. The most popular cyber destinations have figured out how to make money with your content by placing ads around sites like MySpace, which is owned by News Corporation. Just as Starbucks sells coffee and Borders sells books by providing a comfortable place to meet or relax, new e-hotspots attract visitors by engaging customers with intriguing virtual dialogues on every area of life.

What's wrong with that? Potentially nothing and potentially everything. It means more information is coming at us faster than ever from various people who may or may not be truthful or forthcoming with their intentions. It creates new possibilities and new problems requiring shrewdness.

Leading Us into Temptation

Often, the real goal of the half-true propaganda we can encounter online is to lead us into temptation. The "acceptable" line is moving further away from traditional advertising and toward tempting us into sin. The deliberate science of manipulating our baser nature and getting around the guards of our integrity has surged in online popularity.

One trick is to subtly mix in distracting messages to influence decisions. Dr. Baba Shiv, a marketing professor at Stanford University's Graduate School of Business, has demonstrated effective techniques that distract people's cognitive or thoughtful side so that they will be swayed more by their emotional impulses. Dr. Shiv told two groups that they were participating in a memory experiment, but he also offered each of them a choice between a piece of delicious chocolate cake and a healthy bowl of fruit salad. At the same time, one group had a seven-digit number to memorize and the other group received a two-digit number to remember. What happened?

Here's an excerpt from the *CNN Money* article entitled, "How to Lead Your Customer into Temptation":

> Remarkably, 63 percent of the subjects who were trying to memorize the longer number chose the cake, compared with 41 percent of those in the shorter-number group. . . .
>
> Psychologists suggest that consumer decisions are really the outcome of an epic battle. On one side, they say, are primitive emotions such as desire and fear—known as "affective" urges. On the other are higher-order cognitive thoughts, such as "Cake is not healthy. . . ."
>
> The main takeaway from his work, Shiv says, is that—contrary to the fundamental assumptions of traditional microeconomic theory—consumers are far from consistently rational. "When emotions kick in," he says, "people sometimes act against their own self interests."[15]

The study also showed that feeding people suggestive phrases like "chocolate cake has been scientifically proven to be healthy" will influence their decisions. It doesn't matter if the messages are true or false. Although researchers admitted that it would be unethical, dangerous, and probably illegal to use these tactics in the real world, these techniques are used both offline and online today. The hardest part is deciding when the techniques go too far. While merely eating a piece of cake is not sinful, many actions that psychologists call "affective urges" are.

Twenty-first-century appeals to our sin-nature are proving to be effective techniques to make money online. As gambling has grown tremendously in this country and even become an acceptable form of entertainment for many in society, so e-indulgences are spreading as well. Just as sophisticated marketing techniques now package casino visits with popular Broadway shows and cheap travel deals, various cyber temptations are cleverly packaged in new ways that are often difficult to resist because we love "a deal."

Getting Personal

Beyond advertisements, most popular online hangouts have created another world filled with new definitions for what's popular. If you want to thrive in virtual meeting rooms like MySpace and Facebook, it's best to be slender, athletic, twenty-something, and beautiful. Unfortunately, that rules most of us out. No problem, in cyberspace you can be or look like anyone. Just edit your profile—regardless of whether it's true or not. This unspoken new norm is encouraged if you want to compete in the dog-eat-dog fight for digital attention.

Defenders of these actions quickly point out that a little deception is fine, even expected in today's "cybermania," in order to prevent "real-world" problems. Many parents foolishly tell their kids to "stretch the truth" online by saying they are someone else, someone who's eighteen years old, in order to protect their real identity or where they live. These "white lies" actually take away protections afforded to minors. Many websites have extra protections for minors, and undercover police often help ensure that laws are enforced. However, if your twelve-year-old claims to be twenty-one, he/she is subject to a completely different set of rules.

In January 2008, MySpace cut a deal with attorneys-general from forty-nine states to take new measures to protect children from sexual predators through age verification measures. Parents can now submit their children's e-mail addresses to MySpace to prevent them from creating profiles. MySpace also promised to identify and remove pornographic images and links to pornographic sites from its website. Yet critics say that age verification is not an exact science and that there are still many ways to get around the new protections.[16] Richard Blumenthal, the Connecticut attorney general, essentially agreed. His advice was to utilize the new protections but to realize that "no measure is a panacea."[17]

Virtual worlds such as Second Life have created a separate "grid" for underage teens. Again, they try to verify ages, but there are ways to get around protections. The important thing is for parents to encourage honesty with their children regarding online behavior so that they learn that ethics do matter and the laws that are put in place to protect them can work more effectively.

This lying theme is played out in the popular movie *Little Fat Liar*. The character Jayce constantly lies about everything. Someone asks, "Did you eat your oatmeal?" He answers in the affirmative, as we watch the dog eating his oatmeal under the table. We watch as the comedian fools his teachers, parents, and just about everyone else. Throughout the movie, we hear about how "truth is overrated." Lying seems cool. And then . . .

When he tries to tell the truth, his parents don't believe him. Even his friends doubt his integrity. Jayce goes from Michigan to LA to regain his father's trust. Finally, by the end of the movie, we learn the moral of the story: "truth is not overrated."

Still, many people think that small fibs don't really count the same in cyberspace. The case goes something like this: "If I don't want to be a victim of identity theft or sexual predators, I'll just tell everyone that I'm some fictional person." This idea uses the traditional argument that the ends justify the means. Bottom line, everyone's doing it (lying), so what's the problem—as long as no one gets hurt?

Short answer: this creates major ethical concerns, and people are getting hurt. Dishonesty is never a good thing, whether by the CEO of a multinational corporation or a young teenager. If the person writing an online message is a thirteen-year-old student from Michigan who is pretending to be a twenty-eight-year-old teacher from Hawaii, can we trust any person we're chatting with about a difficult relationship? If we redefine cheating and stealing in cyberspace to be helping and sharing, these same definitions will start to show up in real-world schools, businesses, and homes.

Are you still skeptical that this issue is serious enough to require real change? Here are some statistics that may surprise you, from Dr. Michael Conner, a nationally recognized psychologist who has written and spoken about the Internet and the need for crisis intervention:

- 50 percent of the people online lie about their age, weight, job, marital status, and gender.
- Use of the Internet is a contributing factor in nearly 50 percent of all family problems.
- 11 percent of the people going online are becoming compulsive or addicted.[18]

There are endless opportunities to cause mischief in cyberspace. It's so easy to deceive. The Internet is full of false names and descriptions, but are we only fooling ourselves as we engage in various interactions? Nobel Prize–winning scientist Richard Feynman said, "The first principle is that you must not fool yourself—and you are the easiest person to fool."[19]

Are You Addicted to the Net?

One way that we can deceive ourselves is to underestimate the amount of time or influence the virtual world has on our lives. Following Feynman's advice, how can we know if we're spending too much time online? Dr. Conner identifies these questions to ask:[20]

1. Do you feel better when you are online, chatting, or exploring the Net?
2. Are you or have you been spending more and more time online?
3. Are you online when you should being doing something else?
4. Have you tried to cut back and don't?

Another helpful gauge is the time. While some classify addiction as those surfing eight hours or more a day, heavy game users are considered to include those who average more than two hours a day.[21] Kimberly S. Young has described a list of familial, academic, and occupational problems that can result from Internet overuse.[22]

Another expert, Diane M. Wieland, associate professor and director of the Undergraduate Nursing Program at the La Salle University, School of Nursing, Philadelphia, writes that "addictive characteristics, aside from obsessively seeking pornography, may include online gambling, chatting, shopping, stock trading, general information searching, constant web surfing, database searching and an addiction to interactive computer games. Prolonged involvement in these activities can lead to reduced sleep, poor hygiene and lack of physical activity, and certainly indicates compulsive behavior."[23]

While the majority of experts and the American Medical Association refuse to formally recognize "Internet Addiction Disorder"[24]—preferring "web dependency" or "overuse"—others insist that up to 17 percent of teens are addicted in China.[25] In addition, researchers point out that dozens of recognized disorders, such as depression, gambling, and even compulsive lying are played out in new ways online. The Web is sometimes seen as a socially acceptable alternative to recovering alcohol or drug addicts, but many can't properly manage their time and fall back into destructive patterns.

New Meanings for Friendship or Chatting?

Another subtle form of e-deception is judging friendships by quantity and not quality. Ever been asked how many "friends" you have in your circle? Many now measure their social significance by the opinions of others as seen by the comments left on their blog. How quickly we forget biblical wisdom: "A man of many companions may come to ruin, but there is a friend who sticks closer than a brother."[26]

How do you keep surfer friends coming back? I asked several Christian teens this question and visited some of their websites. Although these results may seem mild by some standards, the sites offered illegal music downloads, outlandish claims, and suggestive pictures.

"Don't be so hard on them, Dad. Hardly anyone takes this stuff seriously," was the response from one of my daughters. "I know the difference because we talk about this stuff all the time, but most of my friends don't see it your way. The virtual world is fake to them. None of that really counts. Everyone knows what's really going on."

But the Lohrmann family is not immune to cyber difficulties. One time my daughter Katherine had a cousin over, and they were chatting with former classmates who moved to another state. What started as an innocent IM conversation quickly went downhill and became harsh name-calling with some obscene language. It later emerged that they were communicating with the next-door neighbor of my daughter's friend, who was using his account.

After sincerely apologizing, Katherine made this comment as she looked back at the incident, "What a weird experience! We said things that were not really us. At the time, our actions didn't seem wrong, but it got out of control so fast. That would never have happened in real life. I see how the Internet changed my perception."

There are so many e-messaging traps. People regularly cross the line between innocent fun and creating serious untruths that hurt others and their own integrity.

Two teenage girls in Ohio posted a fake snow day announcement on their school district's website as a prank. Despite no snow in sight or in the forecast, some students stayed home. The girls faced expulsion from school and were charged with crimes. "The company that runs the website, RCH Networks Inc., said the system was not hacked into because no security breach was detected. Administrators say the girls must have somehow gotten the password."[27]

Sadly, there are thousands of stories of "normal people" who enter into dangerous liaisons in cyberspace—based on total deception. Starting with helpful advice or common interests, these double lives often end in tragedy for real people.

In a more serious case, Montgomery, a forty-five-year-old married man with teenage daughters, pretended to be an eighteen-year-old Marine in Iraq named Tommy. "He began instant-messaging 'Jessi,' who later also went by the handle 'peaches_06_17,' and the lies flowed easier with every press of the Return key."[28] A time-consuming online romance began.

Eventually, Montgomery's wife, Cindy, found out about her husband's double life. Although she intervened, the relationship secretly continued. Over time, Barrett, a twenty-two-year-old coworker of Montgomery, tried to warn Jessi that she was chatting with a fraud, but then Barrett fell for Jessi. Many months of trickery and jealousy over Jessi's love unfolded. The real-life soap opera seemed to end when Barrett was fatally shot, and Montgomery was charged with murder.

The ensuing police investigation revealed that "Jessi" was really Mary, a "happily married mom for 23 years." Mary, who was using her seventeen–year-old daughter's—Jessi's—account on Pogo, was reportedly one of the best parents around and a regular cheerleader at her daughter's sporting events. Despite the romantic chat, she denied that she ever loved either Montgomery or Barrett.

After these events, Montgomery gave *Wired* magazine the following explanation:

> When I'm talking to Cindy . . . or you like this, face-to-face, "it's hard for me to say what I feel." As Tommy, however, the words came easily. And then there was Jessi. He loved her, or at least believed he loved her, though he knew he was "never going to meet her." His plan was to "kill Tommy off" in Iraq, but Cindy intervened too soon. He (real-life Montgomery) nearly committed suicide because of his guilt about having lied to Jessi.[29]

Help Online: Finding Trustworthy Sources

If we can't automatically trust what we're reading online, how can we find trustworthy sources? One helpful tip is to follow the librarians. That's right, while many people have forgotten about those physical places in our digital world, twenty-first-century libraries have an abundance of excellent aggregated resources to get to the right answer—not to mention knowledgeable experts who can provide great surfing and other tips.

Can't leave the house or the office? A website called Digital Librarian[30] has chronicled much of what's best on the Web. One nice thing about these sites is that the librarians keep them up-to-date with the latest information. Many digital libraries also provide access to information that would otherwise cost you money. For example, Michigan residents can visit the Michigan eLibrary (MEL)[31] and gain access to periodicals and other information that would otherwise cost them the subscription price. Check your state website for similar offers.

A few other tips: check the sources and references. Wikipedia can range from great to lousy, depending on the author (who can be anyone) and topic, but you can always check the links connected to definitions. You can also check other reputable sources, such as trade associations, university websites, and the websites of authoritative companies (such as Microsoft for computer operating system issues). Finally, check for online versions of reputable print references. While many sources charge subscription fees, others are free.

When you're not happy with search results for a topic, try to ask the same question in a different way or with a different search engine. For example, you can try Ask.com or Live.com instead of Google.com.

Where's My e-Conscience?

Another way that we deceive ourselves is by developing a separate "e-Conscience." Marketing experts recognize that people are often willing to do things online that they would never do if they were faced with the same situation in real life. Similar to how they behave under the effects of alcohol, people are less inhibited on the Internet. For example, people express their thoughts more freely in an electronic chat room than in a grocery store chat. Researchers often call this the "disinhibition effect."

There are numerous, and often complex, aspects to our online behaviors. Dr. John Suler, a psychologist from Rider University, suggests that the Internet brings new concepts to reality.

> Sometimes people share very personal things about themselves. They reveal secret emotions, fears, wishes. Or they show unusual acts of kindness and generosity. We may call this benign disinhibition. On

the other hand, the disinhibition effect may not be so benign. Out spills rude language and harsh criticisms, anger, hatred, even threats. Or people explore the dark underworld of the Internet, places of pornography and violence, places they would never visit in the real world. We might call this toxic disinhibition.[32]

Situations arise online that encourage people to act outside of character. While this effect can bring positive results at times, disinhibition often amplifies online temptation. Internet users change their online language to include four-letter words or use the Lord's name in vain. Schoolgirls are tricked (or bullied) into undressing in front of webcams to get attention. Fictitious stories are told with immoral motives.

I've often seen this online disinhibition change the surfing habits of "good Christians"—even family members—with these behaviors dismissed as just online games, no different than shooting a character in an arcade game. Without much thought, actions are justified by imagining a separate "e-conscience," which adheres to a different set of commandments. Many forget that real people are on the other end of the wire. Gradually, these situations transform our views of right and wrong and spill over into all aspects of life.

What's Your "e-Me" Doing Now?

Examining blatant examples of identity theft, trickery, and illegal deceptions, it is tempting to say, "Not I." And yet, we face more difficult tests in God's world. If we claim to be followers of Christ, we must go deeper and examine our thoughts, motives, and actions.

Screwtape, the senior devil that C. S. Lewis created, described how humans engage in betrayal of God via our actions that slowly change us.

No doubt he must very soon realise that his own faith is in direct opposition to the assumptions on which all the conversation of his new friends is based. I don't think that matters much provided that you can persuade him to postpone any open acknowledgement of the fact, and this, with the aid of shame, pride, modesty, and vanity, will be easy to

do. As long as the postponement lasts he will be in a false position. . . .
All mortals tend to turn into the thing they are pretending to be.[33]

One of my favorite cartoons, which is even a popular T-shirt, pictures a dog sitting in front of a computer while he's talking to another dog. The caption reads, "On the Internet, no one knows you're a dog."[34] Using the cover of online privacy or anonymity, people start living multiple online lives that seem fun and freeing. They become blinded to the lasting impact on their faith and family.

Sometimes people don't engage in blatant dishonest schemes but do mislead others at home, work, or school by spending excessive time online engaged in socially acceptable pursuits. What's wrong with going to travel sites, buying items on eBay, or checking out stock prices? Probably nothing, but are you supposed to be working or studying for a test?

Perhaps the ultimate test of honesty and integrity is to examine how we actually spend our time—both online and offline. Do surfing patterns match up with our professed priorities in life? Are we acting hypocritically? Has our BlackBerry become a "CrackBerry?" While emergencies happen, a constant need to catch up with work e-mails or world events should set off a red flag. Surfing patterns often reveal the true desires of our heart.

Christian Responses

In light of these trends, what are Christians doing differently? Many surfers are joining trusted alternative online communities with likeminded people. This creates exciting places that use the latest technology to engage Christians from around the United States and even different countries and cultures. I list several pros and cons to these websites in chapter 10. From chatting online to e-dating, from virtual hangouts to college-age tours, you can find just about anything with the word "Christian" out front.

But this trend also creates a new set of questions: Who is really speaking? What is their motive? Are they being totally forthright? What are their true values? No doubt, monitored sites that quickly remove inappropriate content provide a very helpful service. If you find a website that you like and trust, spread the word. We need more options to guard against cyber temptations, and the later chapters of this book offer new possibilities in this area.

A growing number of people also go to websites like The Drudge Report[35] or The Huffington Post[36] to get aggregated news from around the world from a conservative or liberal perspective. But be careful, plenty of tempting headlines and stories with questionable links abound there as well. Remember, a comprehensive solution to surfing your values involves people, processes, and technology.

One simple step is to remind ourselves regularly regarding the truth about surfing anonymously. Christians understand the overarching premise that God knows and sees everything. "You know when I sit and when I rise; you perceive my thoughts from afar. You discern my going out and my lying down; you are familiar with all my ways. Before a word is on my tongue you know it completely, O LORD."[37]

Second, we can trust that Christ's promises are true. In the Great Commission, Jesus tells us to make disciples of all nations and teach them to obey everything he has commanded. He ends with this precious promise: "And surely I am with you always, to the very end of the age."[38] If we believe this truth, it will change the way we behave in cyberspace.

What does this look like? How is it different? The virtual world is not just a big game that doesn't count for morality. Yes, pseudonyms are usually fine—and often a necessity. For example: your online name might be "Tigerfan27," rather than Bill. People understand that your real name is not Tigerfan27. Still, pretending to be Sally, a thirty-five-year-old blond from Texas, when you're Alice, a fourteen-year-old redhead from Baltimore, is lying. In the next few chapters, we'll examine other forms of cyber mischief that often thrive in the anonymous world of e-lies.

Third, we must stop and think before we click. Establish good surfing habits and online etiquette. E-mails written in haste or in anger are often regretted. Remember that instant messaging (IM), blogs, and e-mails are written records that are much harder to recover from than verbal miscues. Don't get pulled into an e-mail or IM "war." When in a difficult situation, try to take a short break and walk away from your computer if you can. Better yet, pick up the phone or talk in person when possible.

In May 2007, the *Oakland Press*, a local newspaper in Michigan, published an excellent supplement on safer computing, entitled, "Stop, Think, Click." You can even get a copy of this Federal Trade Commission (FTC) brochure at: OnGuardOnline.gov. While this program limits its focus to stopping fraudulent online practices, I love the "stop, think, click," theme. Using a "real-world" analogy, if you are driving a car too fast and out of control, an accident will surely result.

Put another way, if webpage designers, advertisers, fraudsters, and others are "tempting the click," we definitely need to stop and think before we click. The FTC literature highlights ways to detect scams, but our thoughts at that moment should go way beyond how we might lose money or even our identity. In fact, we are dealing with matters of the soul. Will we sacrifice our virtue, our character, our family, or our faith for whatever they're offering? We need to ask. Might this be the first step down a dangerous road?

Finally, surfing our values requires more than not lying. Silence is often perceived as concurrence with the actions of others—especially in cyberspace. Christian integrity means speaking up with the truth in loving ways. It means being a cyber ambassador for good. It can be hard, and may lead to ridicule, but fighting back for the truth—no matter what the topic of discussion is, is a great way to avoid falling down cyber cliffs.

4 ➡ Do the Ends Justify the Means?

Cheating on the Web

If they'd spend as much time studying (as cheating) . . . they'd all be "A" students.

Ron Yasbin, dean of the College of Sciences at UNLV [1]

It's America's number-one priority. Whether we're discussing standardized test results, local or national politics, career planning, or the cost of college tuition, it's all about education. If there's a topic that liberals and conservatives, spenders and savers can all agree upon, it is this: get a good education and keep learning.

There are plenty of disagreements over the costs and benefits of public versus private education. We argue over which values to teach, whether we should allow prayer in schools, and the need for socialization for homeschooled students. But regardless of viewpoint, parents consistently go the extra mile to get whatever's needed for their children's education. And better education often means the best technology, including new laptops, wireless networks, and access to virtual high schools and colleges.

But what are we teaching about character? The Josephson Institute of Ethics conducted a survey in 2006 of more than 36,000 high school students. Here's an excerpt of the findings:

> Michael Josephson, founder and president of the California-based institute, which does the survey every two years, believes that the students are influenced by adult behavior. . . . "For better or worse, this is the next generation. It is a staggering indictment on parents and teachers."[2]

> Even though more than half of students surveyed said they cheated, 92 percent said they were "satisfied with my own ethics and character." About 74 percent said that "when it comes to doing right, I am better than most people I know."[3]

Americans of all ages are increasingly willing to do whatever it takes to get ahead—even break the rules. In his eye-opening book, *The Cheating Culture*, David Callahan shows how cheating seems to be the "secret weapon" to help people get ahead, or at least keep up.

> We may bowl alone, but we cheat together. . . . Cheating is everywhere. By cheating I mean breaking the rules to get ahead academically, professionally, or financially. . . . Americans who wouldn't so much as shoplift a pack of chewing gum are committing felonies at tax time. . . . Americans seem to be using two moral compasses. One directs our behavior when it comes to things like sex, family, drugs, and traditional forms of crime. A second provides us ethical guidance in the realm of career, money, and success.[4]

Although cheating has always been a problem, Callahan believes the groundwork for our cheating culture was laid in the 1980s in a period he calls "extreme capitalism." Of course, the Internet emerged in the go-go nineties, and a paradigm shift occurred as cyberspace became real for most families. With the promise of more information than ever before just a few clicks away, families happily ordered the latest personal computers for Christmas or birthday presents. Families started to develop the view that owning the latest technology is a twenty-first-century prerequisite to learning, and some recent studies have indeed shown improved test scores by integrating more technology into curriculums.

High-speed Internet is now seen as a "must-have" to support a good education in American homes. Local, state, and national governments have even held conferences to address the growing "digital divide" and help the poorer sections of society keep up with technology. Indeed, it's never been more convenient to become a scholar.

Distance Learning: New Opportunity

From online libraries to virtual high schools, innovative ways to educate others are popping up every day. People are getting degrees from universities on the other side of the planet, and new interactive courses are uncovering more effective ways to teach with threaded discussions via distance learning. Although the exact number of students is disputed, several mega-universities around the world now boast hundreds of thousands or even millions of virtual students, thanks to the Internet and correspondence courses.[5]

No doubt, the Internet is great at connecting students and teachers. Apple Computer offers podcasts of lectures from schools around the country via iTunes U.[6] Students from all over the world now take courses via Norwich University's online master's program in information assurance.[7] Being a "guest lecturer" previously required travel around the country. But over the past several years, I have lectured and interacted with students in Guam while sitting at home in Michigan under the banner of Norwich University (itself based in the beautiful Vermont mountains). The technology works well and creates wonderful new opportunities for millions of people.

Distance learning can also cut costs, offering new tailored curriculums to those who can't afford the ever-increasing expense of higher education. Many reputable institutions, such as Harvard University, have online programs. Missionary organizations are now training pastors in their native languages over the Internet from the United States.

Technology and the Cheating Temptation

So the list of benefits to online education is huge. But with the global competition and the pressure to succeed, the temptation to cheat has never been greater. The Internet is adding new dimensions to cheating. Back in 2001, at the University of Virginia, faculty cited the Internet as the top societal force leading students to commit acts of plagiarism.[8]

In 2005, Secure Computing Corporation reported that almost 800 websites facilitate online plagiarism—a 10 percent increase over the previous year. Here's a quote from their press release:

> Most of the 780 Web sites describe themselves as "essay banks" and offer digital copies of term papers and essays, some for free and others for a price. The larger plagiarism sites offer tens of thousands of essays on a wide variety of topics. Some of the Web sites even offer to write custom term papers on almost any topic. One site charges $19.95 per page for seven-day delivery, and will cater to the worst student procrastinators by providing "same day service" at $44.95 per page.[9]

Donald McCabe, a professor of management and global business from Rutgers University, has been examining cheating trends for years. His September 2006 survey found that well over half of the graduate students in business and engineering admit cheating, and he thinks the survey numbers are probably lower than reality, since students self-reported.

"I would say at many business schools it is a part of the culture," Dr. McCabe said. "You want to talk rationalizations? I could give you thousands of them: everybody else does it, it's the teachers' fault, you have to do it to get ahead."[10]

Tempted by Life Experience Degrees

How about misrepresenting not just your work to pass a course, but an entire degree? Recently I Googled "degree in engineering," and the top results on the first page included numerous excellent higher-education programs like "Kettering.edu." Examining my options, I noticed several "Sponsored Links" that grabbed my interest. One top choice said, "Engineering diploma—Convert Your Life Experience Into A Diploma Now. Free Evaluation." Their link to "www.belforduniversity.org" was sandwiched between engineering options at Oregon State University and Colorado Technical University in Colorado Springs.

Following this "engineering degree" link led to a very professional-looking website with impressive pictures, advisors available round-the-clock, 72,000 graduates with fully accredited degrees, certification and accreditation from the International Accreditation Agency for Online Universities (IAAOU) and the Universal Council for Online Education Accreditation (UCOEA). The website offered numerous benefits, such as a toll-free number to call, the opportunity to earn a recognized degree or high school diploma based on experience from Belford University within seven days, and free education credential verification service on the phone, among many other features.

After I mentioned this website to my visiting mother-in law, she was curious. We looked through their well-designed website and admired numerous options. Your major, degree level (from high school diploma through doctorate degree), date of birth, year of graduation, grade point average, and other items were all blank fields that could be simply input by the user.

Beulah Williamson decided to apply for a doctor's degree in electrical engineering, asking to graduate summa cum laude with a GPA between 3.9–4.0. Where their easy-to-use online form asked for "life experience which qualifies you for this degree," we put three lines: "I like computers and surfing the Internet and e-mail, I use my toaster and oven on a regular basis, and I care about the environment."

Just two days later, my mother-in-law received this information in an e-mail:

Congratulations, Beulah Williamson!

We are pleased to announce that on the basis of your resume submitted by the Assistant Registrar, the 10-member evaluation committee at Belford University has finally

approved you for a Doctorate Degree. You can now pay
the amount from the link provided below and get your
Doctorate Degree within 10 days from today. Once you make
the payment, you will also be able to access the Alumni
Area of Belford University and get exclusive privileges and
discounts. . . . We congratulate you on being approved as a
Belford University Graduate and wish you all the success in
your future endeavors.

Experience Evaluation Committee, Belford University
Belford University | 5715 Will Clayton #1301 | Humble |
TX | 77338

Belford University is just one of many websites that could potentially mislead Web surfers. While I understand that these websites are legally protected under "freedom of speech" laws, the potential for surfers to be deceived is immense. They may offer nice gag gifts, but thousands of people likely submit real résumés and believe these degrees will get them a job.

In reality, there is an abundance of questionable credentials available online. It may be helpful to think of the problem in the same way as you deal with forged checks or counterfeit currency. The entire education system is hurt by this trend.

A recent report by ADP Screening and Selection Services revealed that 44 percent of applicants lie about their work histories, 41 percent lie about their education, and 23 percent falsify credentials or licenses. We're not just talking about the straight-out-of-college crowd either. "Just ask Dave Edmondson, the former CEO of RadioShack who was sacked in Feb. 2006 when an investigation by the *Fort Worth Star-Telegram* turned up overstated academic qualifications."[11]

Online experts in deception often claim to offer services from someone certified in a trade, a personal trainer, a massage therapist, even doctors or pastors, but these people produce false credentials. In fact, if you search on the word "fake" and add just about any profession or other object, you will be shocked at the results showing how widespread this problem has become.

There are thousands of stories with sad endings, such as doctors, senior executives, and clergy exposed as frauds. In many cases, careers are ended or reputations ruined because someone needlessly padded a résumé. In September 2005, a woman in Hong Kong was even sentenced to twelve months in jail for falsifying her credentials.[12]

Of course, the "diploma mill" problem is not new. The Internet simply makes it easier than ever to acquire a fake degree or other very questionable credentials. So what are some ways to spot the fakes?

Spotting a Fake—Simple Steps

With so many worldwide options, how can you authenticate a university? There are some very easy ways to detect a fake institution of higher education online. First, look for the ".edu" extension at the end of the Web address (or URL), for example, www.valparaiso.edu. The ".edu" domain is tightly administered through procedures from the U.S. Department of Commerce by an organization called EDU-CAUSE.[13] While there are some good education-oriented websites with ".com" domain names (and others), be very careful if the university or community college itself has a non-education home address.

The Federal Trade Commission (FTC) has an excellent website that can help ensure that an academic institution is legitimate and help spot a bogus degrees and credentials.[14] Describing the $200 million industry in false credentials, other reputable websites, such as the Online Education Database,[15] provide guidance and excellent searchable information regarding distance education. Baker's Guide to Christian Distance Education[16] is another helpful resource in the search for good online Christian education options.

The reality is that cheating, in whatever form, can be a temptation for everyone. Of course, we rename it with phrases like "cutting corners." Some justify cheating with arguments like: "I knew the material anyway, but I was just too busy to finish the assignment on my own." Others deceive themselves by going to helpful websites like www.Sparknotes.com (which boasts 60 million page-views per month) or www.cliffsnotes.com to get free study guides, but they fail to ever read that Shakespeare assignment or really learn the required material. You can even download notes or frequently used test questions to your video iPod.

Adults that place their résumés online also risk plagiarism. While Americans have become accustomed to using services like Monster.com for ongoing job searches, résumés have been copied by others. Bob Rosner, author of the syndicated column "Working Wounded," described one of these situations in a letter he received in November 2006: "Amazingly, twice in the last month, I have been given my own resume to review with someone else's name at the top. In both cases, the job duties, descriptions, even the project names match exactly."[17]

For this reason, I advise people to make their résumé available only to those who truly need it during a job search process, and not widely available to everyone online. If you want to place your biography on a personal webpage or blog site, omit specific project details that make your résumé more valuable to others. In addition, you can do an Internet-wide search on sections of your résumé to see whether it or other works are being copied by others.

Caught in the Act! Now What?

Some schools and universities have responded to this new normal with a strong stance regarding academic integrity. Consider this story from the University of Georgia:

> It was late, she was tired, the foreign language paper due the next morning was nowhere near being ready—and the information the UGA student needed was there for the taking on the Internet. Drag, click, copy. She figured her professor would never know the difference. Scroll, click, paste. She was wrong.
>
> The work, to put it bluntly, was too good. Confronted by a student solicitor trained to investigate cases of possible cheating, the student, a senior, admitted her plagiarism and took the penalties recommended by her professor: an F in the course and a two-year notation on her academic transcript, which could tell the world—including other universities, post-graduate programs, and prospective employers—that she had been found in violation of UGA's academic honesty policy.[18]

While tough penalties certainly change the risk equation for cheaters, few believe that enforcement alone will work. Besides, not all cheating is created equal, right? At Rutgers University's Center for Teaching Advancement and Assessment Research, a comprehensive website breaks down multiple levels of academic integrity. "Academic freedom is a fundamental right in any institution of higher learning. Honesty and integrity are necessary preconditions of this freedom."[19]

Rutgers recognizes four different violation levels, ranging from "Working with another student on a laboratory or other homework assignment when such work is prohibited" to "Having a substitute take an examination or taking an examination for someone else."[20]

While many schools have rules on cheating, enforcement is often lacking and violators try to dodge personal responsibility. When caught, the responses can get "interesting." For example, in June 2004 a British university threatened to rescind a student's grades for cheating. His response: the university was negligent for not stopping his plagiarism. Michael Gunn claimed that he did not know that his "cut and paste" techniques were a problem. He sued the university for not stopping his cheating earlier.[21]

While the majority of people will not formally blame others for their mistakes or go to a diploma mill for a fake degree, these examples illustrate the extent that people will go to cheat in education. In November 2007, two men were indicted in California for using their computer access as staff on a help desk to change university grades. While this may seem like a movie theme or mild crime to some, the men face felony charges including identity theft, conspiracy, and wire fraud. They may face up to 20 years in prison and fines of up to US $250,000.[22]

Christian Cheaters—An Oxymoron?

Is this trend affecting Christian schools and students? An interesting blog written by a professor at Milligan College began with this heading, "News Flash: Christian College Students Cheat! (But Maybe

Less than Others.)"[23] Professor Jim Dahlman argues that Christian colleges aren't perfect but do offer an alternative model.

There seems to be a noticeable difference, especially in the smaller Christian schools with tight-knit communities. "My sense would be that the more the school is infused with its Christian heritage, the more it teaches Christian principles, the better it will be,"[24] said Donald McCabe, from Rutgers Business School.

When I was at Valparaiso University in the early 1980s, we had an honor code that is still in effect today. I remember the pledge that we wrote on every assignment, quiz, and test: "I have neither given or received, nor have I tolerated others' use of unauthorized aid."[25] At Valpo, exams are taken without proctors walking around looking for cheaters. This creates a different environment overall, where the goal is not to beat the system or outsmart the teacher, since friends and other students usually know more about the intentions of their classmates than do teachers.

> The basis upon which the Honor System at Valparaiso University is founded is in every way consistent with the highest principles of ethics and morality and presumes that students are able and willing to accept the duties and responsibilities for maintaining the principles of honorable conduct for the sake of the community and themselves.[26]

Quite a few secular and private colleges and universities have implemented honor codes, as do the military academies. But few K–12 schools use honor codes. At a minimum, honor codes ensure that everyone is regularly reminded of the rules and writes the honor code on each assignment. In response to Dahlman's blog, one person wrote:

> I cheated a couple of times in (Christian) high school but never in college. Several factors contributed to my repentance:
> - I was raised to see cheating as wrong.
> - I learned my lesson about cheating in HS. I was never caught, but I was ashamed of my actions and realized that I missed out on learning because of it.

- I committed my life to the lordship of Christ after my freshman year in college.
- My college, Rice University, had an honor code. On every assignment, I had to hand-write on the front "I have neither given nor received aid on this [assignment/test]."[27]

A closer look at this response provides several elements that I believe are essential in combating the powerful temptation to cheat, whether in school, at work, or online.

1. A genuine understanding of right and wrong. This could also be called your school policy, workplace rules, ten commandments, or code of conduct.
2. Recognition and repentance for past mistakes (may include punishment).
3. Faith in God and belief in ultimate justice, accountability, and blessings for obedience.
4. Written "honor code" that enforces standards on a regular basis. This opting-in to honesty and integrity on all assignments and exams is paramount and powerful.
5. Family, friends, coworkers, leaders, and others who share your values and provide encouragement and accountability.

While these guidelines may seem too simplistic, if you believe these statements are true, you have the core requirements needed to surf your values in the future. Of course, this doesn't deal with the technical specifics of academic integrity, but as I will describe in later chapters, new mechanisms to help are coming.

Help for Parents and Teachers

As we move deeper into the twenty-first century, there is no doubt that education is undergoing a radical transformation as a result of the Web. There are many excellent organizations that are heavily engaged in promoting character and academic integrity, and preventing cheating in America. The Josephson Institute initiated the "Six Pillars of Character," which are trustworthiness, respect, responsibility, fairness, caring, and citizenship.[28]

One message that the Josephson Institute teaches in its courses on ethics is that parents cannot be "values neutral." An extensive number of free resources are available to parents at their Character Counts website. A roadmap for parents to talk about integrity and character with their teens can be found under the tab "Academic Integrity."[29] These programs are supported by thousands of schools, businesses, communities, public agencies, and nonprofit organizations.

Ironically, online degree programs tend to do a better job at detecting and preventing students from cheating than do many traditional teaching situations. By using new grading mechanisms such as student interactions on personalized questions, Norwich University's master's program is able to offer the benefits of a global faculty, without as many of the temptations for students to cheat. These new approaches force students to provide real-life answers from their personal work experiences and enable other students to ask follow-up questions and engage classmates in a deeper dialogue called "threaded discussions."

There are several excellent umbrella organizations, like the Sloan Consortium, that are working to improve distance learning and ensure academic integrity. When it comes to providing quality online education, the Sloan Consortium's purpose is to "help learning organizations continually improve quality, scale, and breadth of their online programs, according to their own distinctive missions, so that education will become a part of everyday life, accessible and affordable for anyone, anywhere, at any time, in a wide variety of disciplines."[30] There is a free level of membership available to all, which provides extensive access to white papers, conferences, the latest research, and online access to over twenty thousand educators to stay in touch with new trends.

The Center for Academic Integrity,[31] at Clemson University, is a comprehensive Web portal containing an abundance of good material for educators. You can purchase an "Academic Integrity Assessment Guide" to determine where your school currently stands in regard to a culture that allows cheating. The guide includes access to a Web-based survey instrument for 500 students and 200 faculty per campus. Once the survey is completed, a confidential report is provided which compares a school's results to aggregate data from students and faculty across the country.

The University of Maryland's University College Center for Intellectual Property[32] provides an outstanding list of services, guides, publications, and stories related to copyright protection. I also like the University of Maryland's Education Technology Outreach Center, which "links research to practice,"[33] covering topics like e-books, courses in cyber ethics, cyber safety, and cybersecurity, lesson-plan templates for teachers, free course downloads, and upcoming events.

A shorter but very practical list for teachers and parents comes from the State University of New York's Web library page entitled Tips for Handling Technology Enhanced Cheating.[34] This site contains practical ways to reduce technology-enhanced cheating, examples of cheat websites, and lists of resources that can help detect plagiarism, such as Plagiarism.org and Canexus.com.

Getting Personal—Biblical Standards

The biblical standards for honesty and integrity are very clear:

> The LORD abhors dishonest scales, but accurate weights are his delight.[35]
> There are six things the LORD hates, seven that are detestable to him: haughty eyes [reflects a proud heart], a lying tongue, hands that shed innocent blood, a heart that devises wicked schemes, feet that are quick to rush into evil, a false witness who pours out lies and a man who stirs up dissension among brothers.[36]
> The man of integrity walks securely, but he who takes crooked paths will be found out.[37]

Dr. James Boice, former pastor and founder of the Alliance of Confessing Evangelicals, told this story as part of his exposition of Psalm 106:24–27—the story of Israel's rebellion against God and Moses in the desert. A teacher was asked the question: "What does the Lord want from me?" The response: "What God wants most of all is to be believed." Dr. Boice went on to say that unbelief is at the root of all sins, and the opposite of unbelief is faith, which is the way of salvation.[38]

In other words, when we cheat (or commit other sins), we are not trusting God's promises. This unbelief manifests itself in the myriad of ways that we try to maneuver in our online lives. We act as if we know what is best—and rebel against God's Word. When faced with a cheating culture, what do we need more of? Faith. Jeremiah 17:9–11 (NIV) says:

> The heart is deceitful above all things and beyond cure. Who can understand it? "I the LORD search the heart and examine the mind, to reward a man according to his conduct, according to what his deeds deserve." Like a partridge that hatches eggs it did not lay is the man who gains riches by unjust means. When his life is half gone, they will desert him, and in the end he will prove to be a fool.

No matter what wonderful technological advances we implement in the twenty-first century, we will always face this underlying challenge of the desires of the heart. The "people issues" will always be paramount, because there will be ways to cheat in every situation. As Christians, our faith and trust in God enables academic integrity.

5 → Identity Theft and Integrity Theft

Partners in Crime

We live precariously on the knife-edge between chaos and control. What was once an open space between law and freedom, one governed by character and truth, is now deserted, so law must now do what character has abandoned.

David F. Wells[1]

In August 2007, the State of Michigan faced a clever new form of cyber attack. E-mail boxes started filling up with messages containing the subject heading "e-Card from your daughter." The simple text message: "Hey dad [or mom], check out this e-Tune." This new spam was actually an ingenious method to infiltrate our network defenses by tempting users to click on a link. After analyzing what protections we employed, the attackers were able to use just a few characters to bypass our state-of-the-art spam filters (which already blocked over 90 percent of the e-mail sent into state government).

Unfortunately, it worked. Almost 200 state employees clicked on that link, which secretly established (unseen) connections to overseas computers that tried to infect their PCs with viruses and steal personal information. But in this case, "Batman" came to the rescue. Our security experts, who work in a restricted area we've nicknamed the "Bat Cave," were monitoring incoming and outgoing network traffic. Alarms started going off, notifying us of numerous unexpected communication attempts to Asia. Our team blocked the unauthorized Internet addresses and prevented any loss of sensitive data. They notified those who clicked, and got technicians to fix their PCs. Unfortunately, for most home users, Batman never comes.

How could this happen? Our expertly designed protection scheme was fine-tuned to find the professional-looking spam that pretends to be from banks, insurance companies, or eBay. We had trained state employees not to click on these types of e-mails, but we became a victim of our own success. We had stopped spam messages so successfully over many months that when this simple new spam got through, many state employees took the bait.

Similar lessons in social engineering are repeated millions of times each year at homes and businesses around the world. When one attack method fails, the bad guys try another exploitation technique. Just as football coaches try to call the right defensive play to stop the opposing offense from scoring, security staff defend computer systems. But this is not a game, and it keeps going.

You've Got Mail

Just a decade ago, America fell in love with e-mail. Meg Ryan and Tom Hanks portrayed life in 1998 in the romantic comedy *You've Got Mail.*[2] Americans of all ages held their breath when the online question was asked, "Do you think we should meet?" Since e-mail was still a novelty to most, this new technology added suspense and intrigue to this unlikely relationship. How quickly things change.

As a fun and revealing exercise, try renting the movie again and compare the people, processes, and technology used in the 1990s with Internet life in America as we approach 2010. Warning: your kids will probably think Kathleen Kelly (Ryan) and Joe Fox (Hanks) lived in the Dark Ages.

Without doubt, the pendulum has now swung in the opposite direction, and we are no longer excited by the simple message "You've got mail." According to a 2007 IDC study,[3] nearly 97 billion e-mails were sent every day in 2007, but over 40 billion of those were spam messages. That number is almost certainly low: the Messaging Anti-Abuse Working Group (MAAWG) estimates that 80–85 percent of incoming messages were "abusive email," as of the last quarter of 2005.[4]

While we complain about this e-mail deluge and the backdoor tricks, Americans continue to click. Shrewd imposters imitate our friends, business partners, and extended families. Let me be clear: the number of unwanted messages will continue to grow in the near-term, because they work. Just as illegal drugs flow into our country, wherever there is a demand, there will be supply.

But where are the lines? Defining the problem is hard, because one person's spam is someone else's free invitation to a seminar, monthly newsletter, 30-percent-off discount coupon, or other benefit. The reality is that we each face the daily challenge of deciphering whether the motive of the sender is genuinely friendly, an immoral trap, or even illegal identity theft. Many get so fed up with the process that they shut down one e-mail account and open up another one with another company. But of course they soon face the same deluge of spam at their new e-mail address.

Legislation to allow citizens to opt out of spam has been largely ineffective, for many reasons.[5] It has become a worldwide problem for law enforcement. Fortune 1000 companies and a never-ending list of coalitions have joined the fight to stop organized crime and other cyber bad guys. Still, we're outgunned and playing defense. Occasional victories, such as the arrest of the LA Botmaster,[6] are far outnumbered by regular defeats, and new spam quickly fills the previous void. What is absolutely clear is that new solutions will again require action and opting-in, such as e-mail "white lists,"[7] from end users.

Understanding the Cyber Frontlines

At an important 2007 meeting assessing the threat of spam, Deborah Platt Majoras, Chairman of the Federal Trade Commission (FTC), described some of the negative results that can result from simply clicking on a link in a deceptive e-mail message:

> You may be lured to a website that will either trick you into divulging your personally identifying information, or infect your computer with spyware or other types of malware. Even merely opening a malicious email can subject you to harm from malware. The surreptitious deployment of such malware can result in slowed computer performance; installation of key-logger software that can record and report your every keystroke; the spread of computer viruses; and the hijacking of your computer for use as a botnet. [A botnet is a collection of software robots, or bots, which are run remotely as "zombie" computers—usually by bad guys.]
>
> In addition, new threats to communications media other than email are knocking on the door. Spam's cousins, SPIM (spam over instant messaging), SPIT (spam over internet telephony), and spam to mobile devices, threaten to undermine the benefits of mobile services and Internet telephony in the same way as spam. Social networking websites have become yet another frontier for spam messages.[8]

What do the bad guys want? The answer is almost always cash. Cyber crime is the fastest-growing criminal activity in the world, because it is a high-reward, low-risk occupation. Table 3 lists the items that Symantec Corporation has found available as commodities on the black market, along with an indication of what percentage of the "underground market" those items represent.

In a June 2007 press release, the FBI announced over 1 million potential victims of botnet cyber crime.[9] Another way that we know these cyber crimes are becoming more frequent and easier to commit is that the value of personal information is actually going down as a result of high availability of the information. As shown in Table 3, personal information from credit card numbers to bank account numbers to Social Security numbers (along with name pairs) is available for sale on the black market.

Rank	Item	Percentage	Range of Prices
1	Credit Cards	22%	$0.50—$5.00
2	Bank Accounts	21%	$30—$400
3	E-mail Passwords	8%	$1—$350
4	Mailers	8%	$8—$10
5	E-mail Addresses	6%	$2/MB—$4/MB
6	Proxies	6%	$0.5—$3.00
7	Full Identity	6%	$10—$150
8	Scams	6%	$10/week
9	Social Security Numbers	3%	$5—$7

Table 3. Breakdown of goods available for sale on underground economy servers. Source: Symantec Corporation[10]

Totally Random Attacks? Think Again

While it is natural to feel like you are "just a number" in this global cyber war, attacks are no longer simply random. With the growth in social networking sites like MySpace, Facebook, and LinkedIn, which are full of personal information, a new trend has developed. Cyber threats are increasingly targeted or personalized. The *Wall Street Journal* told one victim's story:

> An email landed in the inbox of Scott Foernsler, head of global sales at Air2Web Inc., an Atlanta mobile messaging and marketing company. It informed him that a Better Business Bureau complaint had been filed against him and asked him to click an attached link to respond.
>
> The email featured the Better Business Bureau's familiar torch logo running across its top on a blue background. It addressed Mr. Foernsler by name and also provided the name of his firm as well as a case number. The sender's email address: consumer-complaints@bbb.org.
>
> The email looked so professional that Mr. Foernsler, an executive with 22 years of sales experience, never suspected a thing. "Anything about our customers I want to take action on," he says. He clicked on the link and was informed he would be contacted again.[11]

Scott was later sent another e-mail saying that the complaint had been dropped, but he never suspected anything suspicious until he was informed that his computer was infected. A security company traced the infection to clicking on that link. He never found out how his personal information was being used. In mid-September 2007, MessageLabs, a security firm, uncovered over 1,100 such e-mails sent in a sixteen-hour period.

Despite these scary attacks, the credit card companies have effectively responded to the situation by adding numerous protections. As long as you check your bill each month and report fraud promptly, you are generally well protected. But in response, the bad guys have also adapted, and they steal more than just credit cards, from a wider array of targets. Consider this case:

> Cyber thieves broke into computer systems at Convio, a marketing company for nonprofit organizations, and stole email addresses and member passwords from 92 organizations, including the American Museum of Natural History and CARE. . . . Convio discovered the intrusion on November 1, preventing the attackers from stealing information from 62 other clients. No credit card information was compromised in the intrusion.[12]

Sadly, there are even people who want to steal identities of the dead. By obtaining the names of the deceased, and the dates of birth and death from obituary columns, the identity thief can search the Social Security Death Index (SSDI) and find the Social Security number. The information can be used, for example, to open new credit accounts. That is why the FTC wisely recommends getting a credit report on a recently deceased loved one to identify all open accounts. Then notify all account holders of the death, as well as insurance companies, the state agency responsible for driver's licenses, the fraud departments of the three credit reporting agencies, and the Social Security Administration. (More recommendations can be found at www.FTC.gov.) Finally, be careful about information available in the obituary. You can include the year of birth, but the birth date and place of birth of the deceased could become problematic.

Everyone's Afraid of the Big Bad Wolf

Worldwide public awareness campaigns have successfully alerted the public to the "big bad wolf" of identity theft. The constant barrage of attacks is simply incredible. Since 2005, the Privacy Rights Clearing House has kept track of the approximate number of records that have been compromised due to security breaches.[13] (This is not necessarily the number of individuals affected, since our personal records can be in multiple places, from banks to department stores.) As of November 2007, the number was well over 215 million in the United States, and counting. The technology industry, financial institutions, and the criminal justice community have become painfully aware of the various forms of identity theft.

Initially, many banks and others feared that warnings via commercials and flyers in monthly statements would scare people away from online banking and thereby cost them even more money, but no longer. Flyers with helpful tips are now commonplace from financial institutions, and if your credit card is used fraudulently, the liability has dropped from $50 to $0 in most cases, if you report promptly.

Many experts saw these problems coming over a decade ago, but persistent efforts to effect change began in about 2004. These are very serious issues that demand serious action. We now face many more years of important work, but at least we have the public consensus and the financial incentives needed to get the identity theft problem fixed.

Identity theft, privacy, and cyber attacks are now priorities for governments around the world. To protect yourself right now, you can consult dozens of great websites, articles, and books on security and privacy topics. In Michigan, our governor and attorney general have created two award-winning websites[14] that can help teachers, parents, businesses, and individuals with questions in these areas. These sites also point to many other great resources available on the Internet that can help with security and privacy. You can even get a free DVD from the U.S. Treasury Department on how to prevent personal ID theft.[15]

One encouraging development for consumers is the emergence of insurance covering identity theft. Michigan's five largest home insurers started to offer some form of identity theft insurance in 2007. "AAA extended the coverage at no additional charge to some policy holders—others ask consumers for a fee to add the coverage."[16] While this coverage can't prevent ID theft or the pain associated with recovering from the ordeal, at least the financial impact is lessened.

Getting Personal about Cyber Theft

While so much negative attention flows toward illegal activities like identity theft and online predators, other unethical and immoral conduct quietly eats away at personal integrity in cyberspace. There is no doubt that getting caught committing a cyber crime and showing up in the paper will immediately expose a lack of integrity and ruin one's reputation, but most people never face that music. In fact, shocking cyber crimes tend to offer a smokescreen for just about everything else that's troublesome in cyberspace. Just as a comparison with Hitler will make anyone look good, we excuse lesser trespasses by comparing ourselves with the worst predators and thieves.

Meanwhile, there is an explosion in personal shenanigans in cyberspace that many are reluctant to label as "stealing." Illegal copying of digital music, movies, pictures, electronic books, and other items is rampant. While there are plenty of websites that advocate the view that everything digital should be free, local, state, and federal governments continue to call copying these items and distributing them to others theft. The "digitally free" argument goes something like this:

> No matter how many people the RIAA [the record industry] sues, no matter how many times music executives point to the growth of digital music, we believe an increasing majority of worldwide consumers simply view recorded music as free. . . . A new model for music consumption must emerge and that model most likely involves DRM-free downloadable music at no cost to consumers, fully supported by advertising.[17]

In my experience, this illegal activity is very common among Christians. While many parents worry about the implications of suggestive pictures their teens view online, they don't seem to care much about the hundreds of illegal downloads available from the same sites. If they caught their son or daughter stealing even a candy bar from the corner drugstore, there would be severe consequences. However, they see nothing wrong with thousands of dollars' worth of stolen digital merchandise being shared with friends online. Many aren't aware of the extent of the problem—and some parents are doing the same things, even burning CDs full of their favorite music and handing out copies to friends and family at parties.

How did we get to this point? Some of the problem may be the result of a lack of understanding of laws. The "everyone is doing it so it must be okay" argument is rampant. But there are a million ways to justify inappropriate actions. Just as people justify cheating on their taxes because they think taxes are too high, Americans have developed a code of conduct in cyberspace that has very little to do with the actual law.

Others don't understand the implications for the music industry or how this hurts artists and writers. Most professionals can't sing or write "for the fun of it." Our country has a long history of respecting intellectual property rights, and in my view, this issue is actually black-and-white. Consider these numbers:

> According to the U.S. Commerce Department, intellectual property theft is estimated to top $250 billion annually (equivalent to the impact of another four Katrinas), and also costs the United States approximately 750,000 jobs, while the International Chamber of Commerce puts the global fiscal loss at more than $600 billion a year. But both estimates appear to be woefully underestimated; by some other estimates, there was over $251 billion worth of intellectual property lost or illegal property seized in August 2005 alone.[18]

Cyber Termites: How Moral Decay Leads to More Crime

While there are many ways that people justify their cyber activity, table 4 demonstrates how individual Internet conduct ultimately works to create the serious personal impacts that feed societal cyber crime. While most of us may prefer to talk about the Third World hackers and the serious problems listed under the second column, far fewer people understand how their personal conduct impacts the wider situation on the Internet. More importantly, these activities undermine your personal and family integrity, as discussed in the previous chapters.

Cyber Activity	Personal or Family Impact	Business or Societal Impact
Clicking on a phishing scam, infected e-mail, or e-card trick	Lost information and credibility, inconvenience, false sense of security, later mistrust	Identity theft, cyber crime exploding into multibillion-dollar problem affecting law enforcement, government, and business
Plagiarism—illegally copying material	Stealing, lack of learning, inflated grades, guilty conscience, discipline, expulsion	Academic integrity questioned, unfair grading, more cheating leads to mistrust of schools
Downloading copyrighted songs, movies, DVDs, etc.	Redefines stealing, personal lawsuits, home viruses and worms, opens Christians to charge of hypocrisy	Corporate lawsuits, hurting music and movie industries, billions lost in sales, theft overwhelming, viruses, worms
Christians consuming porn, visiting inappropriate websites	Violates trust and vows, leads to addictions, lust, adultery, fornication, divorce, harms marriage, hurts ministry and reputation	Violates work rules, hurts productivity, leads to escalation of violence and child porn, societal degradation, degrades women, hurts families
Providing false name, age, location	Lying, reduced trust in online transactions and chat, loss of protections provided to minors, easy deception, loss of key relationships	Internet protections fail, easier to commit crimes, lack of identity controls, more complexity, sexual predators attack
Falsifying qualifications and credentials on résumés, stretching the truth on skills	Reputations damaged, guilt, loss of job, career impacted	Human resource decisions undermined, professionals lack qualifications, jail time
Misrepresenting the facts on products we sell, value of items	Lying, buying the wrong items, hurts trust	Hurts growth of online sales and overall economy, limits online possibilities, FTC crimes for false advertising
Inappropriate relationships, saying things that are unkind, bullying, lack of etiquette, online manners	Helpful chat rooms become emotional and spiritual problems, relationship issues, marital mistrust or divorce	Relationships weakened, online predators

Table 4. Cyber Conduct—Personal Consequences Lead to Societal and Criminal Impact

A quick glance at the chart shows that even while most of us never have a run-in with the law or are even questioned regarding acceptable use policies at work, our lives are much more deeply affected by what illegitimate activity does online than we realize. Whether people are overtly or covertly tempted into engaging in these acts, the results affect every aspect of life. At an elementary level, this chart is common sense. For example, if everyone started physically robbing banks, we would have a huge surge in crime that law enforcement couldn't stop. The amazing thing is that this surge is now occurring in cyber crime without the majority of society realizing what's happening or the impact.

On the other hand, this list may seem odd in some ways, since it includes actions we can label as deliberate cyber sins (such as lying, cheating, stealing, and lust) as well as inadvertent acts like being tricked into clicking on a phishing scam.

Yes there are innocent victims of scams. But just as often, sins of omission are later evident. While it can be counterproductive to draw too many lines around various cyber temptations because they typically feed off each other, many Americans justify one or more of these activities. For example, our kids have grown up in an Internet culture that encourages them to forward tempting e-mails or other messages based upon novelty, not truth or benefit. This lack of discernment becomes a feeding ground for cyber criminal to "tempt the click."

So what am I suggesting by way of response? If we want to establish respect for the laws affecting cyberspace, it must start with the small things. Just as mayor Rudy Giuliani's actions dramatically curtailed violent crime in New York by hunting down and stopping low-level crime, we need to transform the Internet one person at a time. Giuliani reportedly said New York needed to

> dispel cynicism about law enforcement by showing we treat everyone alike, whether you are a major criminal or a low-level drug pusher. . . . A city should be a place of optimism. Quality of life is about focusing on the things that make a difference in the everyday life of all New Yorkers in order to restore this spirit of optimism.[19]

The crackdown on the "squeegee men," who previously demanded payment for cleaning car windows, became a huge victory.

Cleaning up graffiti and trash also helped establish a new normal. The primary focus of the police changed from responding to crime to preventing crime. Despite skepticism, the mayor's policing innovations led to historic drops in crime—with total crime down by 64 percent during the Giuliani years. The number of cars stolen in New York City went down by 78,000 per year.[20]

As Christians exemplify the fruits of the spirit, honor their marriage vows, and obey the Ten Commandments, they strengthen their personal situations and reduce online crime at the same time. How? Those who live with integrity are much less likely to engage in the cyber activities listed in table 4. As we surf biblical values, we also lower the risk of being tempted to visit websites that could compromise our integrity. More on this topic is found in chapters 7–10.

Skeptics might respond by asking: What impact will my personal behavior possibly have on the huge Internet? What impact can one family really make? Of course, the same arguments are made in every area of life. Just as millions around the world are paying extra to "go green" and help save the environment from global warming, cyberspace is actually the aggregation of millions of individual connections. Every little bit helps. More importantly, I'm convinced that once a certain threshold is reached, crime can be reduced in the same way it was in New York. For these reasons, the primary answer to our criminal problems turn back to better training, personal conviction, and ethical behavior in cyberspace.

Virtual Fun but Real Crime

Even as we bring our real-world values and integrity more consistently into the virtual world, we need to be aware of just how sophisticated the virtual world is becoming. Cyberspace now offers new virtual worlds with a countless number of fun things to do. Habbo Hotel is one popular online world/community/game where new players create an online character (called a Habbo) that represents them. "People can come to relax, hang out and make friends in a safe, non-threatening environment."[21] The game is free to register and check into the hotel, but extras such as club membership, diving in swimming pools, and room furnishings can be bought with "Habbo Coins," which are purchased with real-world money.

According to the BBC, six million people in more than thirty countries play Habbo Hotel each month. In November 2007, a Dutch teenager was arrested for allegedly stealing virtual furniture and moving it into his own hotel room. A spokesman for Sulake, the company that operates Habbo Hotel, said: "The accused lured victims into handing over their Habbo passwords by creating fake Habbo websites. In Habbo, as in many other virtual worlds, scamming for other people's personal information such as user names has been problematic for quite a while."[22]

Business Week is one magazine that has watched the growth of online worlds very closely. Consider this story: "A perpetrator with privileged information hacked into a stock exchange's computers, made false deposits, then ran off with what appears to be the equivalent of $10,000, disappearing into thin air."[23]

None of this transpired in the real world. The robbery took place in Second Life. There are now virtual companies courting your avatar's business. Some of these companies are listed on virtual stock exchanges, where their shares are bought and sold by avatars with "Linden dollars" and other virtual currencies that can be converted into U.S. dollars or other currency. Thousands of Linden dollars are bought and sold each day.

While the creators of these virtual worlds fight the type of regulation required by real banks, there is little doubt that some regulation is coming. Why? As these virtual worlds grow, millions of dollars and euros will ultimately be exchanged into virtual currencies (backed up by real-world currencies). According to Wikipedia, the exchange rate for Linden dollars was stable at $266 to one U.S. dollar in February 2007;[24] however, Google advertisements offered many different prices for the virtual currency.

The bottom line is that virtual worlds are becoming big business. While many Second Life players insist they are just participating in a fantasy game, real money will bring real regulation.

In a recent abrupt move, Linden Labs outlawed all gambling in Second Life,[25] due to the unwanted attention that they were starting to get from law enforcement agencies. When the policy change was announced, many real-world companies issued press releases to shareholders that explained how they are complying with the new rules.

New Businesses, Virtual Tycoons, and ID Theft

In November 2006, Ailin Graef, sometimes called the "Rockefeller of Second Life" became the first personality to achieve a net worth exceeding one million U.S. dollars from profits earned entirely inside a virtual world. Ailin's avatar is named Anshe Chung. Her achievement was remarkable, "because the fortune was developed over a period of two and a half years from an initial investment of $9.95 for a Second Life account."[26]

While Ailin Graef's story is remarkable, thousands of other cyber entrepreneurs are close behind her with similar success stories. As these new virtual worlds thrive, more money is invested in cyberspace every day. Most large technology companies are setting up virtual headquarters, and major investments are being made in Second Life by Fortune 500 companies. IBM announced an investment of $10 million in 2006.[27]

But with the virtual money come the virtual bad guys. Promises of anonymity and privacy put your personal identity and your integrity at risk in new ways, and your online reputation is connected to your avatar. If someone steals your avatar, they've essentially committed virtual-world identity theft. Besides the fact that many people invest large sums of money and time to build up their image and reputation in cyberspace, even "borrowing" someone else's avatar has huge implications beyond money and power. What if they go into chat rooms and say things you would never say? What if they go to virtual destinations and perform immoral acts? Bottom line: the issues surrounding integrity theft in these massively multiplayer online games (MMOGs) are becoming just as compelling as the issues surrounding real-world identity theft.

Symantec believes that malicious code will become much more pervasive and sophisticated in MMOGs such as World of Warcraft and Lineage.

Although most MMOGs are designed to be played by players, automated tools can be used to enhance play and avoid some tedious, repetitive activities. The downloading and use of these tools presents an opportunity to attackers to incorporate malicious programs such as keystroke loggers and password and information stealers, which the user may unknowingly install on their computer. . . .

Users in these environments may receive emails that claim to be from a game's administrators that direct users to spoofed Web sites that are designed to capture account information, such as the player's username and password. The phisher will thus have access to the legitimate player's account, from which they can then distribute the player's assets to other avatars, or sell the account to another player.[28]

An Avatar in Your Future?

You may care very little about playing online games, no matter how lifelike they seem in 3-D. You may never imagine yourself spending time in a "second life," especially when it often seems there's not enough time for your "first life" in the real world. Even if these are your feelings, I recommend some awareness of MMOGs. These and other virtual worlds are rapidly expanding. The technology research firm Gartner forecast that by the end of 2011, some 80 percent of active Internet users and Fortune 500 companies will have a "second life" in some sort of virtual world (though not necessarily in the Linden Labs' Second Life).

During these initial years, when all of the bugs are getting worked out of these new virtual worlds and the rules are being established, Gartner recommends that companies follow "five laws" when participating in public virtual worlds/platforms:

1. Virtual worlds are not games, but neither are they a parallel universe (yet).
2. Behind every avatar is a real person.
3. Be relevant and add value.
4. Understand and contain the downside.
5. This is a long haul.[29]

I think Gartner's recommendations for business provide wise pragmatic advice that is also very relevant for individuals. Gone are the utopian dreams that these new worlds created online will be "perfect," without the fear of any prejudice or crime. Any heaven coming to earth won't be arriving in cyberspace.

At a very basic level, parents need to know where their kids are going online and whom they are interacting with in these virtual worlds. As pointed out in "law" number two, behind every cool, interesting character online is a real person whose motives are unknown. There are many stories of people who met in virtual worlds who are intrigued to the point of acting out in real life.

David O'Berry is a technology director and an Internet expert from South Carolina who has been an active online participant in several "massively multiplayer online role-playing games" (MMORPGs), including Second Life. O'Berry sees the societal impacts of our new e-morality. I interviewed him to further explore these trends.

> I've seen it all. It can be fun or really frightening at times, because even people that I know in RL [real life] can act completely different with their avatars in cyberspace. They take on different personalities. Quite honestly, they carry out actions that, were they done in the physical world, would make them cringe, but they justify their actions by saying it's just a game. Couple that issue with how easy it is to become addicted, and this new virtual community has ruined real lives and impacted the family members folks love most, in many situations.[30]

Some adults who would normally avoid porn sites or adult content engage in immoral activity in virtual worlds. They justify this because the scenes are artificial. The common justification: "It's just a game. These are cartoon characters." Don't be fooled into immoral situations, which inevitably lead to further trespasses in other parts of cyberspace. Just as Gartner's business-world advice points out, these liaisons will inevitably lead to somewhere—and not always somewhere good.

I believe that when it comes to virtual worlds, "we ain't seen nothing yet!" Just as spaceflight simulators are used to train pilots, we will enter virtual reality to learn new techniques at work, test-drive new cars, try on new clothes, experience a concert, or simulate real-world public reaction to upcoming political speeches. These new worlds will appeal to us, create a sense of urgency, and provoke a need to act. The temptation to click will never be greater, but we won't need a mouse—just a verbal command will do. Or, perhaps someday, just a thought.

Getting Personal—An Online Risk Assessment

Hopefully, one thing is clear after reading this chapter. We are all vulnerable to the big bad wolf of identity theft, that sly fox, the on-line predator, and the harder-to-see cyber termites that undermine our virtue and integrity and lead to more cyber crime. As we travel through cyberspace, it is helpful and necessary to occasionally pull over and make sure we're going in the right direction and doing the right things. I think of this as a personal online risk assessment.

As I've said, I believe the technology side of the risk assessment is actually the easiest part of this puzzle. At the absolute minimum, we need to ensure that our computers have an antivirus software package loaded and running with up-to-date virus signatures (files that detect and stop the latest threats) before connecting to the Internet. Symantec (Norton) and McAfee have excellent products that come with built-in spyware and botnet detection and other essential security features, such as personal firewall protections. I also strongly recommend adding filtering and accountability software, which I cover in chapter 8.

Beyond virus and firewall defenses, we need to implement a security or privacy checklist and examine recommended best practices from trusted websites. I'll mention three portals with excellent checklists:

OnGuard Online—www.onguardonline.gov
"Provides practical tips from the federal government and technology industry to help consumers guard against Internet fraud, secure their computers, and protect personal information"

Stay Safe Online—www.staysafeonline.org

"Sponsored by the National Cyber Security Alliance (NCSA) to promote safe behavior online"

The NetSmartz Workshop—www.netsmartz.org

"Educational resource material for children and teens"

The United States Computer Emergency Readiness Team (US-CERT) website maintains a reading room[31] with easy-to-use implementation guides like: "Before You Connect a New Computer to the Internet."[32] Other helpful US-CERT publications, which are available for free in the reading room, include: "Protect Your Workplace," "Recovering from a Trojan Horse or Virus," "Home Network Security," and "Software License Agreements: Ignore at Your Own Risk."

Like regular visits to your dentist, semiannual visits to these helpful websites ensure one is taking the appropriate technical steps based upon the current threat situation. These sites offer plenty of free advice, Internet training, interesting videos, fun quizzes, webcasts on hot topics, online newsletters, links to report frauds and security incidents, and many easy ways to ask questions. On a more regular basis, remember that help is almost always available from the leading Web portals. For example, Monster.com has help (see http://help.monster.com/besafe/) on how to keep information safe when using their services or putting a résumé or biography online. E-Harmony, eBay, YouTube, Facebook, and many other sites also offer advice.

Taking a huge step back, we must never forget that the integrity theft battle is, at the heart, a spiritual one. In chapter 3, I mentioned a quote from C. S. Lewis's classic book *The Screwtape Letters*. A senior devil instructs a junior devil in the art of tempting humans. Screwtape's letters to his nephew Wormwood provide invaluable insight that makes the entire book a must-read. Consider these other bits of relevant devilish advice:

> You will say that these are very small sins; and doubtless, like all young tempters, you are anxious to be able to report spectacular wickedness. But do remember, the only thing that matters is the

extent to which you separate the man from the Enemy. It does not matter how small the sins are provided that their cumulative effect is to edge the man away from the Light and out into the Nothing. Murder is no better than cards if cards can do the trick.[33]

We have trained them to think of the Future as a promised land which favoured heroes attain—not as something which everyone reaches at the rate of sixty minutes an hour, whatever he does, whoever he is.[34]

Don't believe the lie that small sins don't matter much. "Sow a thought reap an act, sow an act reap a habit, sow a habit reap a character, sow a character reap your destiny."[35] The future starts right now. As Steven Curtis Chapman sings in one of his famous songs, our challenge is to live the next five minutes faithfully. Once we do, we "start it all over again."[36] It may sound easy, but in cyberspace, everything moves even faster—including temptations.

6 ➡ This Is Looking Like Work

How Cyber Ethics Impact Your Business and Career

Watch constantly against those things which are thought to be no temptations. The most poisonous serpents are found where the sweetest flowers grow. Cleopatra was poisoned by an asp that was brought to her in a basket of fair flowers.

Charles Haddon Spurgeon[1]

Just over a decade ago we didn't even have Internet access at work, but now we can't live without it. Surfing the Net is now an expected perk in most offices in America. It's fast, it's fun, and, best of all, it's free. Or is it?

Worldwide trend watchers call it "online oxygen."[2] A Websense Corporation survey discovered that it's now as crucial to the workplace as coffee.[3] Once plugged in, many workers become addicted. The new unspoken view: as long as you avoid the "sinful six" (pornography, gambling, tasteless sites, hate material, violence, and illegal activities), you can surf anywhere else online. Just get your job done, and don't get caught breaking any rules.

Road warriors are connected in greater numbers than ever, with powerful tablet PCs and convenient new phones that double as computers. In one form or another, Americans stay connected, and we're proud of it. U.S. workers are the most productive in the world,[4] and the Internet and new technology are a big part of our success.

Some never disconnect. On one end of the spectrum, a growing number have a very difficult time turning off work. Keeping up means 24/7 availability, so we carry a BlackBerry (sometimes known as a "CrackBerry" for its addictive qualities) or other devices wherever we go. Whether at home before bed, walking through malls on weekends, on vacations, even at church, we need to stay current with the latest developments. Can't sleep at night? Might as well get up and read e-mails.

There is even an online forum devoted to telling heroic (yet funny) stories of crazy BlackBerry owner antics. One guy dropped his in the water while fishing in Florida and dove in to retrieve it. Another accidentally threw his away and searched for hours through a dump site for his lost "berry." Others lost their precious device out the window while driving or searched the house for hours to find their missing gem.[5]

Of course, most people don't think of this new normal as a problem. In many professions, this "level of commitment" is now expected. Staying connected equates to staying relevant or staying positioned for the next promotion. "No longer the pitiable drones and graspers of society, today's overachieving professionals are recast as road warriors and masters of the universe."[6]

We think we're in control, but is cyberspace controlling us? Consider this story from the *London Times*:

A recent global survey by the Centre for Work-Life Policy, a New York-based nonprofit group, found that 45% of executives were "extreme" workers, putting in more than 60 hours a week and meeting five other criteria such as being on call 24 hours a day and facing demands from several time zones and meeting ever more demanding deadlines.

Some 65% of men said their work stopped them having a strong relationship with their children. The same was true for 33% of women. Intimate relationships suffered, too. The study found people referring to "four in a bed" relationships—two people, two Blackberrys. At the end of a 12-hour day 45% of all respondents said they were too tired to say anything at all to their partners.[7]

No matter how many hours you work per week, most feel pressured as they watch others always getting ahead. Pastor William D. Hyatt from Peninsula Bible Church in Cupertino, California described twenty-first-century pressures and how they affect our identity and priorities:

> While you're at your desk, people working out in the gym are getting ahead of you. While you're at the gym, your coworkers are getting ahead of you. If a friend gets a promotion at work, she has gotten ahead of you. If a colleague reads a book you haven't read, he has gotten ahead of you. . . . [You] always judge yourself, and your intrinsic moral worth, in terms of specific achievements as compared to others. [You] always judge any situation in relation to how much the people involved have gotten ahead of you, and in what ways.[8]

Multitasking Becomes Telcvisiphonernetting

To keep up, we multitask. Our twenty-first-century answer is to mix work, play, and even family time. This new reality is hilariously illustrated by a Comcast cable advertising campaign launched in 2007 to sell high-speed Internet, phone service, and cable TV as a single package. Picture this: a family is watching a football game together, only Dad seems to be lost in a daze, as he also has a portable computer on his lap, and a phone to his ear. The family tries to explain to Grandpa that their dad can't hear or see them because he is "televisiphonernetting," or watching TV, talking on his phone, and surfing the Internet at the same time. The elderly man snaps his fingers and waves his hand in front of his son's face to no avail. "He can't hear you, Grandpa," is the message from the teenagers.

Like many other ad campaigns today, these "triple play" commercials can be seen at Comcast's website,[9] and they get customers engaged by having them send in words that they create. Words like "snurfing," which means surfing the Internet and talking on the phone at the same time, are more than just a funny fad. Recent studies suggest that more of us are combining activities as never before, and our attention spans are getting shorter as a result. "Eighty-two percent of respondents merged another activity with their web browsing, and 23 percent managed to juggle four or more activities while online."[10]

But it also works the other way around. Home life is now showing up at work like never before. As shown in diagram 1, activities can provide business benefit (bottom row) and personal benefit (top row of rectangles), or be security problems (middle row). According

Diagram 1—From My Work PC

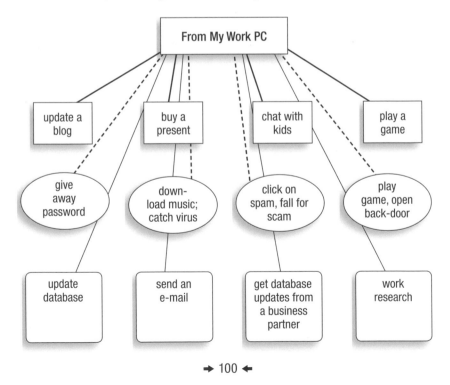

to a 2007 Salary.com report, U.S. workers are "wasting 20 percent of their workday."[11] The top time-wasting activity is surfing the Internet and sending personal e-mails, followed by socializing with coworkers, conducting personal business, and just plain "spacing out." All of this loafing is supposedly costing employers $759 billion a year in lost productivity.[12]

Workplace Monitoring—Or Not

Despite company policies that often forbid personal Internet activities, staff are shopping, playing fantasy sports, chatting with friends, and much more. Regardless of work policies forbidding various activities, most people now view a nominal amount of surfing as an expected perk with work equipment, especially if they are putting in long hours or traveling.

A U.S. Department of the Interior (DOI) audit report stated that agency employees were spending thousands of hours a week visiting shopping, sex, and gambling websites. The 2006 report looked at only one week's worth of DOI computer use and turned up more than a million log entries in which some 7,700 employees visited game and auction sites. During this one week, 443 employees accessed sexually explicit sites. "Our findings suggest that the equivalent of 50 full time staff (FTEs) spend all their work hours surfing Internet on-line game and auction websites over the course of a year . . . at a (potential) cost of $2,027,887.68 per year."[13]

While this DOI report may seem rather incredible, most governments and businesses around the country are dealing with similar situations. Why don't you hear about this topic? Governments are required by law to share audit findings with the public, but most companies do not share this type of information or their cyber battles with the public. No doubt, many organizations do stop egregious behaviors with filtering software, but every large organization struggles with these problems. Despite improving software and recognizing the problem, the situation is likely to worsen—unless we set a new course.

Many wonder why these behaviors are often swept under the rug and not addressed appropriately. At the root, we are judging moral and ethical conduct that company management, and especially human resources, technology, and security staff, are loath to address with the workforce. Unless laws are clearly being broken or companies face a lawsuit, cyber ethics is an area that can get uncomfortable for most professionals in our postmodern world, where I'm okay and you're okay.

So, while most security professionals I know love to talk with kids about not downloading copyrighted movies or talking with strangers online, we are less eager to address (legal) adult behaviors at work that violate company policies. Unless it brings down an operational network, unethical conduct is a topic that management, like security professionals, typically wants to avoid. While it is fairly easy to draw lines, the tough question becomes, How do you enforce lines? What's really happening?

There are dozens of reasons for this, but here are a few of the frequently heard (but unspoken-in-public) excuses that managers give for not addressing cyber ethics at work:

1. Not my job. Managers point to tech staff to solve problems, techies point to supervisors, everyone points to human resources.
2. I might get in trouble. Some supervisors have been accused of being on a "moral witch hunt." For example, "Did she really cheat or lie?"
3. Doesn't get you promoted. Easier to ignore. Overheard: "That's a personal matter."
4. Higher priorities and bigger fish to fry. We need to stop cyber crime and protect sensitive information. Leave personal e-mails, shopping, and chat alone.
5. Just try to block the really bad stuff, and move on. We don't want any adverse morale issues right now. [Do you ever?] We cut bonuses, so let them surf.
6. For government staff only—the inappropriate use reports (on employees) could be subject to the Freedom of Information Act (FOIA), and later public scrutiny, so don't produce them.

7. Guilt. Haven't you ever crossed the line? Are you innocent? Ever done Christmas shopping at work or violated another work policy?
8. It's been going on for too long. Why stop it now? Besides, no budget or staff for issues.
9. Keep company out of the papers. Don't want a legal fight.
10. We need to recruit more young ("Generation Y") employees. They expect to surf freely.

Some managers don't come to these seemingly pragmatic conclusions right away, but over time they get worn down, and the above-mentioned attitudes often set in. Many supervisors can tell a war story or two of how they tried to hammer cyber ethics (or whatever your company calls it) at some point over the past decade, only to be thwarted by executive leaders or HR personnel, with "Back off a bit and send us only the worst offenders." Despite written policies defining acceptable use, everyone is struggling to keep up with the latest fads and challenges, like MySpace, YouTube, dating sites, etc.

One related (but seemingly opposite) trend: whenever a supervisor is "too eager" to convict an employee for Internet indiscretions, a red flag goes up in the minds of security investigators. I've seen managers try to get rid of employees they don't like (for whatever reason) by getting security to do "the dirty work." These managers don't want to discuss poor performance with staff or deal with attitude or relationship issues, so they attempt to remove them by blaming their surfing habits. The reality is that cyber forensic investigations[14] acquit employees as often as they convict them of wrongdoing. Perhaps a virus took over their PC and caused a problem, or maybe they've done nothing wrong.

Still, one colleague from a major consulting company told me that the "inappropriate surfing" problem was so bad in their company that they just stopped all Web filtering, with the exception of blocking viruses and spyware. Their new approach: leave it up to the individual employees to ensure that they just "took care of business and didn't end up in any of the wrong places." The reason: they wanted to remove any motivation for staff to attempt to go around filters and try to outsmart company cyber police. This amounts to a dangerous "don't ask, don't tell" policy.

Personal Freedom versus Legal Risk

Two powerful, yet opposite, cultural forces are now working at the same time at the office. On the one hand, employers are prone to let staff surf as long as the work is getting done and no one complains. On the other hand, organizations are facing new challenges and compliance regulations and court orders from e-discovery lawsuits that enable anything digital to be used in civil proceedings. For example, personal e-mails at work now show up in divorce proceedings.

Think about the policies at your company. Are you permitted to chat, play games, write blogs, shop, or watch videos? What happens when personal chat and e-mails become inappropriate? What if the company is faced with a court order, harassment lawsuit, or hostile work environment based on one of these letters showing up at the printer?

These are just a few of the tough questions involving cyber ethics in corporations and government. Company management gets pulled into personal situations by the police when users break the law—such as online solicitation of minors—but there are many, many cases that never reach that threshold. In general, most experts are too busy stopping cyber criminals to worry about who is flirting with whom online at work. Yet it clear that there are real costs from online abuse in the workplace. Some of the impacts related to poor cyber ethics at work are listed below.

1. Visiting social networking sites increases the risk of cyber crime. Cyber criminals often visit these sites to gather personal information on individuals to help them with their evil intent.
2. Inappropriate behavior is more likely to bring in viruses, bots, illegal software, etc. As people download files and click on bad links, the security risks increase.[15]
3. Loose cyber ethics can contribute to a hostile work environment.

4. Incidents can create teamwork problems when not dealt with properly by management. Coworkers notice and resent this behavior.
5. There are legal ramifications for businesses as employees engage in unauthorized activities. Many types of information are protected by laws such as the Health Insurance Portability and Accountability Act (HIPAA). Many compliance laws contain specific dos and don'ts for company employees, and taking online risks can open up companies to lawsuits.
6. Concerns about staff productivity result.
7. Public and/or stockholder expectations of fair, ethical, and open government or business are eroded or violated.

Are You for Us or against Us?

The computer industry has created sophisticated processes to analyze how "human vulnerabilities" now lead to organizational risk. Organizations pay consultants to conduct studies with scoring factors such as the attractiveness of a target, the frequency and length of time that people are available, the susceptibility of staff, and how easy it is for a cyber attack to be conducted. Once these vulnerabilities are scored, protections (or mitigating factors) are accounted for before determining the level of overall risk of a successful attack. (For example: one mitigating factor is to run a criminal background check prior to hiring staff.) There is no doubt that having employees with excellent character is more valuable than ever; the challenge for businesses and governments is to determine who is who.

While detailed studies have been done regarding external versus internal cyber risk,[16] the reality is that external "bad guys" are using social engineering as never before to tempt internal workers into helping them with their dirty work. The result: harm to both the individual and the business.

The National Association of State Chief Information Officers (NASCIO) addressed this problem in a 2007 white paper entitled, "Insider Security Threats: State CIOs Take Action Now!"[17] To address the situation holistically, NASCIO broke the workforce into two broad groups—those with malicious intent and employees that are just inattentive or complacent in their roles (see table 5).

Individuals with Malicious Intent to Cause Harm	Individuals Who Are Inattentive (Non-malicious Intent) or Complacent
The IT Expert with a Hacker Mentality	The Tech-Savvy Employee Who Gets around Security Measures
The Dissatisfied or Disgruntled Employee	The One Who Just Doesn't Pay Attention—Can be technology or business staff
The Terminated or Demoted Employee	The Untrained New Guy
The Fraudster Motivated by Financial Gain	The Employee without Adequate Training
The Employee Who Wants Unauthorized Access to Information	Others??

Table 5. Insider Threat Motivations[18]

How can we address these threats? The NASCIO report and other documents from The SysAdmin, Audit, Network, Security (SANS) Institute[19] identify the need for oversight (trust but verify), training employees (technical and process-oriented training are offered), and even ways to address visitors and contractors who enter and leave organizations quickly. Most attacks perpetrated by insiders don't just come out of the blue. The Computer Emergency Response Team (US-CERT) found that 80 percent of insiders exhibited "concerning behaviour" prior to attack, including lateness, truancy, arguments with coworkers and poor job performance.[20]

This new world may sound like "big brother" to many staff. Don't end users deserve privacy on work computers? The answer is generally no. Courts have consistently stated that businesses may monitor the computer activities of their staff—as long as policies are clear and consistently applied and proper training has occurred. While most managers want happy employees, there is a job to get done, and online security risks must be taken seriously and addressed properly. Breaches of data and embarrassing headlines have awoken many corporate executives to the importance of protecting their digital assets in a dog-eat-dog world where competitors are constantly seeking any advantage.

No doubt, there are many complicated issues regarding workplace computer privacy, about which we may not immediately agree, but there is no evading the reality that your personal integrity may be at risk when you're surfing the Web at work. How do e-temptations jeopardize your career? Most importantly, what can you do about it?

e-Temptation: Business and Personal Risk

As portrayed in many popular TV shows over the past decade, the business office is a microcosm of society. Every person is unique, and this fact certainly shows up at work. Our different personalities, outlooks on life, likes and dislikes also affect how and where we are tempted. The Internet is our new "edged tool" that can be used to benefit or to wound.

While table 5 addresses broad categories of employee motivations, table 6 digs deeper into how various individuals are tempted online. Of course, these stereotypes are too simplistic, since no profile perfectly matches any one of these darker-side characterizations. And yet, just as Internet marketing teams find it helpful to build different customer profiles to segment their online messages to various audiences, identifying different work profiles may help individuals isolate personal vulnerabilities.

A few assumptions and warnings about table 6: This chart is primarily intended for end users—individuals who are examining their online lives and careers, and not for managers to classify their staff. Despite the negative characterizations here, all of these staff members are achievers with many positive attributes. If an honest self-assessment is done, most people will relate to different characters and the corresponding dangers on the list at various points in their career. Also, the names are in no way supposed to limit the gender of the personality type; for example, "Bored Bob" could easily be "Bored Betty." Finally, I am not suggesting that every tempting activity is always wrong. A modest amount of online shopping at work, for instance, may be fine if your company policy allows it. However, I am suggesting that excesses in each area are a threat to businesses and personal careers in the ways mentioned.

Employee Name/ Description	Tempted By	Threat to Business	Threat to Personal Career
Adventurous Alex—Desperately seeking new buzz, experience	Games, Second Life, traveling sites, virtual world, gambling	Productivity, online reputation, missed deadlines, morale	Lack of contentment leads to downfall, business focus lacking
Bored Blake—Doesn't like his job, not enough to do	Looking for jobs, real estate, cars, auctions, news, etc.	Productivity hit, office morale affected, spreads discontent	Job confusion, disciplinary action, crossing moral lines
Curious Kate—Loves new stuff, surfs for romance, gossip	Updating personal web pages, e-mail, MySpace, Facebook	Company image, productivity, reputation	In deeper than she realizes, wasting time, reputation
Fanatic Fred—Loves sports, reads analysis of games, betting	Sports scores, fantasy sports leagues, chatting, etc.	Productivity, bandwidth, illegal online betting	Never-ending number of games consumed, addiction
Homebound Holly—works from home, watching kids	Home PC for work, mixing home/work, personal business	Spreading viruses to business, losing sensitive info, productivity	Lose the "right and privilege" to "telework"
Traveling Tom—executive, takes chances, "owed" fun	Porn, games, portable devices go around controls	Burnout, example not "family-friendly," hostile work environment	Adultery, jeopardized marriage, faith, family, job
Deserving Debbie—high-producer, earns right to surf	YouTube videos, news sites, how-to portals, you name it	Inadvertent mistakes, knows rules but not risks, bandwidth hit	Proud attitude leads to bitterness at others, deep anger
Naive Nina—student, doesn't realize the rules or the risks	Everything online, illegal downloads, Net is a "right," personal devices	Loss of sensitive info, bypassing traditional defenses to bring in threats, "toys" abound	Reputation, cultural mismatch, getting fired
Savvy Sam—techie, cyber guru, bypasses controls, secret life online, well regarded	Music, movies, porn, challenge to deceive, profit, personal business on side	Lawsuits, copyright violations, bandwidth, hard to find, covers tracks, retaliation	Reputation, arrest, moral consequences, faith, family, career impacted
Lonely Linda—Looking for deeper relationships online	Dating sites, seeks meaning, connects with distant friends, family	Work relations strained, inability to properly view others in office, communication hurt	Goals from personal life hamper work, mind is somewhere else, focus lacking
Greedy Greg—focused on money-making schemes	Stock quotes, Wall Street, eBay, hot tips, deals	Productivity, not focused on his work and tasks, lawsuits	Hurts promotion prospects, bad reputation, fired
All of the Above—Signed work policy on acceptable conduct	Going places online that they shouldn't go during work	Viruses, scams, bad publicity, security breach, integrity theft	Relationships with coworkers, managers, company

Table 6. Employee Stereotypes of Temptations and Resulting Business and Personal Risks

As you examine your work situation, some basic questions can help you decide whether you have online integrity problems:

1. What would happen if my boss and/or company president or division director knew everywhere I surf online and for how long? Can I defend my actions?
2. What if my pastor, spouse, or trusted coworkers discovered my actions?
3. Will I view my surfing habits as a positive or negative five years from now?
4. Are my actions honoring to God?
5. Is my behavior helping or hurting my company?

From a Judeo-Christian perspective, there are definite dangers on both extremes listed within table 6. On one hand, I've seen the Internet act as a trap that disqualifies outstanding performers. There are millions of people like "Deserving Debbie" who do great work but fall into one of the many traps that await them in cyberspace. Thousands of pastors, lawyers, doctors, professional office staff, and computer gurus can attest to this fact: great work is not an excuse for inappropriate actions.

On the other hand, simply obeying workplace rules and laws does not, by itself, make someone a good employee or guarantee career success. Most workers have legitimate business to conduct online, and everyone comes across temptations when they enter cyberspace even for strictly professional purposes. The key is to understand the threats to your career and the business, to stop and think before you click, and to realize that your surfing reflects and affects your integrity.

An open, honest discussion with your boss regarding the Internet can provide a healthy balance. Unfortunately, in my experience, that type of conversation is pretty rare in workplaces today, even if you have a good relationship with your management. In some cases, the boss is the worst offender in the office. In those situations, I recommend talking with reputable security staff or a trusted friend or an executive you respect.

Conscience with Coursework

Surprisingly, many employees take greater risks online at work than at home. According to the Information Systems Audit and Control Association (ISACA), which polled 301 white-collar workers at companies of at least 100 employees, "35 percent had knowingly violated a corporate IT policy. . . . More than 90 percent told ISACA they considered their offices secure."[21] The survey also showed that most people think someone else is responsible for taking care of security on their work computers, and that even if mistakes are made, nothing bad will happen to them.

Another survey of government employees found that despite 97 percent of them taking some type of awareness training and most being aware of the right things to do, "only about 20 percent of government workers follow prescribed security policies all of the time."[22]

Despite recent efforts to educate employees on Internet dangers, the situation is getting significantly worse. The focus of new campaigns must include individual responsibility, accountability, and, most of all, defense of personal and corporate integrity. Christians need to examine their actions at work, not just from a "top-down" corporate-ethics or policy-compliance perspective, but from biblically based obedience and from a desire to work out the implications of their faith.

I will go one step further and suggest that an essential role for current "faith at work" programs around the country must be to assist staff in meaningful ways to surf their values and to live out the implications of authentic faith. Governments and businesses will benefit by encouraging faith-based opportunities to exhibit character online, but in no way discriminate against any religion or belief. While this topic will make some at the office uncomfortable, many others will breathe a sigh of relief and proclaim "At last."

In his book *God at Work*, David W. Miller, who is the executive director of the Yale Center for Faith and Culture, examines how the faith at work movement is positively impacting corporate ethics today. "Hundreds of thousands of women and men around the country have come to feel an urgent need to integrate their faith and their work."[23] Miller provides evidence of an authentic social movement that is growing with a diversity of members and modes of expression. He provides examples of how the role of faith is growing in business life.

This new push will be a win-win situation for both security and privacy advocates as well as for individuals who want to integrate genuine practice of their faith at work.

What's Your Google Rep?

If you're looking for a new job, you'd better check your "Google Rep" (or online reputation). Before you're ever invited in for an interview, most employers now look to cyberspace for information about you. Some use what they see to test an applicant's honesty. "Eighty-three percent of recruiters . . . said they used search engines to learn more about job candidates, according to an Aug 2007 survey released by the recruiting firm ExecuNet. Furthermore, the number who had eliminated a candidate based on what they found online jumped from one quarter (25 percent) to nearly one half (43 percent)."[24]

Employers are even demanding respectable conduct from avatars that represent you. "IBM has issued a series of 11 Netiquette guidelines for workers that spend time in SL and other virtual environments where they might interact with the public."[25] So what's the new expectation? Even when not at work, employees must remember: "Protect your—and IBM's—good name." Staff should assume that all activities in virtual worlds and in the 3-D Internet are public. Therefore, all actions should be consistent and truthful, and protect privacy, and IBM staff must report inappropriate actions to human resources.

These new virtual expectations bring wide-ranging public responses. In the comments section at the end of the *Information Week* article, "Sensible Sue" said, "IBM's 'Netiquette Guideline' should be an example for developing virtual businesses, corporate or not. As in real life, there is a time and place for everything. The success of business in Second Life depends on its ability to evolve beyond its hedonistic reputation and casual approach to life."

"JoePro45" retorted, "Sorry Sue, Where SL has gone wrong is that they let it become a tool for 'real' world business instead of maintaining the 'virtual/fantasy' world that many original 'vertizens' signed on for. . . . Trust me, the more regulations, restrictions, and rules from the 'real' world become applicable here the faster it'll crumble into a 'virtual' vacuum . . ."

What JoePro45 doesn't yet understand is that SL and other virtual worlds affect your real-world integrity. Not only is this big business with billions at stake, there is virtual advertising with metrics measuring your avatar's activities.[26] Just as off-field activities count in professional and amateur sports, ethics count both offline and no matter where or when you travel through cyberspace.

Losing the Enterprise to Marketers

Already losing the battle to keep up with the never-ending array of new online temptations, corporate enterprises need to prepare to face a new wave of workplace challenges. As streaming video applications become even more compelling to employees, as more bandwidth is diverted to nonproductive purposes, and as new devices and new workers enter the workforce, another struggle is just starting to appear. In exchange for cheap or discounted services, get ready for constant commercials on just about every possible Internet device.

Microsoft and Google now offer "free" office applications that they will even run for businesses on their servers. One example is "Gmail." So businesses save millions and get free word processing, e-mail, spreadsheets, perhaps even free database access and storage of files. The catch: just watch (or listen to) the ads. Of course, Microsoft and Google make their money by selling the Internet ad space to other companies. The cost model is very compelling, especially to those who can't figure out how to filter Web ads, anyway.

But who controls the tempting messages that hundreds of millions will be seeing? What is deemed "acceptable"? Google says they will "do no evil," but who decides what is evil? What is their moral standard?

If the answer is "just trust us," be concerned. No doubt, their initial approaches are rather conservative to get companies to sign on, but eventually, the values of even Microsoft and Google will be tested by offers from companies that are willing to pay big to gain unfettered access to millions of eyeballs around the globe. Make no mistake, the pressure for most businesses, which are already being forced to cut costs every day, will be too great. Even federal, state, and local government employees will become captive to viewing whatever is built into this new experience to save dollars. At stake and now being negotiated: the moral integrity of end users. Our virtue is now a pawn in this multibillion-dollar chess game.

Advertisers understand the power of Internet marketing far better than the rest of us. They entertain, make us laugh, target specific groups, and get results. They know if a new ad works. If it doesn't work (meaning no one is clicking), they quickly adapt.

So this raises questions. Where are advertisers, those paying for cyberspace, turning to implement values? How are they planning to tempt us? If we can't beat them, can we please join them in determining what's acceptable? Can we make a deal? If we get this wrong, the Islamic headscarf debate in Europe[27] will seem mild when compared to the new cultural battles in the American workplace. We need win-win approaches that allow employees to surf their values.

While this analysis sounds negative toward Microsoft and Google, I am not necessarily opposed to this new reality. But as company executives make important decisions regarding the outsourcing of these technology functions, they must consider more than the security and privacy implications of the data. They must consider the virtue and integrity of their company and their employees in a new world where cyberspace is not just a great sales channel but also an essential staff tool.

Think Tank Answer: Withdrawal

So what advice is coming from global consultancy experts? Almost every expert acknowledges that office networks are merging into the global bubble of cyberspace. The difference between internal and external threats is quickly blurring. As employees bring in new devices like smart phones and USB drives and plug them in at work, the "consumerization" of office networks is making important security tasks almost impossible.

Recognizing that office life is changing fast, Gartner now recommends a managed withdrawal from the desktop, mainly for security and privacy purposes. A May 2007 report tells executives to stop managing what doesn't need to be managed, by creating separate environments for users and a new secure perimeter for sensitive data that needs to protected. "This research describes how consumerization and manageability can be reconciled by reducing and eliminating enterprise presence on user devices."[28] The benefit: if users surf into trouble and their system gets compromised, the data is still locked safely away.

The report went on to say, "Users will accept lockdown of the corporate image only if they also are provided with an unmanaged space for their own digital assets."[29] A related report states that Gartner clients voted to reject tight control over users.

And Gartner is not alone. The flood of powerful new gadgets entering workplaces, which ZDNET calls the "commoditization of hardware,"[30] is bringing new dangers into work and forcing management to rethink policies. Having lost the battle with staff, companies are starting to welcome "Christmas presents" (such as personal storage media, powerful cell phones, or even home computers) into work.[31] But while this approach is a pragmatic answer that addresses an out-of-control situation, it ignores many of the complex legal and political questions. What happens when this "unmanaged space" is used to commit crimes? Will the business be held liable for not monitoring employee conduct? More important, will this really work?

Not only will this approach present additional productivity and bandwidth issues for companies, this managed withdrawal deserts loyal employees in the intensifying moral battles in cyberspace. Granted, many employees want to be free to surf wherever they want, but is that really an ethical practice? Regardless of my opinions, parts of corporate America are heading in this direction.

Perhaps an analogy will help describe my point. The movie *Black Hawk Down* describes the events which led to a U.S. military pullout of Somalia in the early 1990s. Once the military protection was gone, chaos broke out in the streets of Mogadishu.

While this new freedom from "military rule" may seem nice to some, employees in settings where management create a second unmonitored computer space must get ready to take on the virtual warlords of Mogadishu by themselves once the figurative U.S. Marines pull out. The cyber battles at home and work will essentially merge together for many.

Another Response: Enterprise Ethics

Others in the business world who have considered these perplexing issues don't believe companies can afford the withdrawal strategy. They point out that cyber ethics is just another form of communication and a subcomponent within business ethics. Business organizations, including governments, are very sensitive about their reputations, and dirty tricks that fool others are usually exposed by bloggers and eventually come back to hurt. Likewise, the actions of even lower-level employees are impacting stock prices and political campaigns.

With four out of five worldwide companies affected by fraud,[32] many organizations are starting to address workplace ethics in new ways. In addition to running more background checks and testing employees in ways that predict integrity,[33] companies need to offer training that dispels myths about ethics and brings complex cyber issues out from the shadows. Consider the results of a recent study that debunked many ethical management myths:

Myth: It's easy to be ethical.	Fact: Ethical decisions are ambiguous. Most will be influenced by peers' and leaders' words and actions.
Myth: Unethical behavior in business is simply the result of "bad apples."	Fact: Most people, including adults, are followers when it comes to ethics. When asked or told to do something unethical, most will do so.[34]

The Word of Mouth Marketing Association (WOMMA) recognizes the importance of ethics in how they market products and services. The essence of the WOMMA Ethics Code comes down to the Honesty ROI:

- Honesty of Relationship: You say who you're speaking for.
- Honesty of Opinion: You say what you believe.
- Honesty of Identity: You never obscure your identity.[35]

The WOMMA website also has an Ethics Assessment Toolkit, Ethical Blogger Contact Guidelines, and an Ethics Adoption Toolkit.

Along similar lines, the Shrewd Enterprise portal[36] challenges each of us to answer the question, Are you a shrewd worker? This excellent resource has almost a hundred articles and research studies on ethics alone, as well as hundreds more on risk and other vital workplace issues. Important topics include teaching ethics, redefining success, even how "Poor Work Ethics Risk Future of US Business, Education and Ultimately Freedom."

One article quotes Proverbs 18:9: "'He who is slack in his work is a brother to him who destroys.'" The words hit me like a thunderbolt. Why? Well, I have been guilty of being slack in my work sometimes. I know you have too. The writing on the wall is clear: if you are lazy or slothful, then there is no difference between you and a person who destroys or wastes."[37]

Your Soul at Work

In Sir Thomas More's famous address to Richard Rich at the end of *A Man for All Seasons*, the courtroom was silent as Sir Thomas spoke these words: "Why, Richard, it profits a man nothing to give his soul for the whole world—but for Wales?" The stakes are just as high for each of us. Will we sell our soul for an experience in cyberspace?

In a world where *Business Week* reported that approximately 70 percent of all Web traffic to online porn sites occurs between the traditional work hours of 9:00 and 5:00,[38] where "hacker kits" are bought daily on eBay, and where the majority of staff are violating policies without thinking twice, it is important for companies to look deeper at what's really going on. The easy answer is to issue more "speeding tickets" or hold "public hangings" (that is, discipline acceptable-use violators). While I agree that some of that is needed, there must be a balanced approach between management's role in educating employees and staff members taking personal responsibility and maintaining accountability. Employees can no longer wait for management to solve the problem, because it ultimately comes back to personal character, virtue, integrity, and other heart issues.

7 ➜ Just Do It

Creating and Maintaining Virtual Integrity

The mighty doors of change swing on the tiny hinges of discipline.

Ken Wendle, Co-founder/past president,
IT Service Management Forum (itSMF) USA

Lost opportunities in life come at home, work, or school. One resource management consultant said it this way:

> Contrary to popular belief it is not poor judgment, or lack of resources that is the main killer of businesses. The leading business killer is procrastination. Putting off until tomorrow, next week, next month, or next year has killed more ideas, innovations, improvements, and human initiative than all other faults combined. Procrastination is a chronic malady that lingers on and on. It drains individuals of vitality, robs organizations of opportunities, strips people of income, and causes the premature death of careers. It is the destroyer of positive ideas that could become realities, but remain forever fiction because of inaction. The insidious methodology of procrastination is death through delay.[1]

It is easy to minimize the impact of doing nothing. Being comfortable with the status quo, we are tempted to persist in staying put until something "breaks." But we vastly underestimate the risks of staying put. It takes wisdom to decide when to apply which adage—"If it ain't broke don't fix it" or "The early bird gets the worm." Still, when it comes to change, we tend to dawdle.

The "just do it" theme, made popular by Nike, is often the immediate push, the positive incentive, the kick in the pants that I need to get downstairs and exercise, get my taxes done, or simply take out the trash.

So how can we "just do it" and get started with online integrity in cyberspace? If applying filters is not enough, what are the essential disciplines we need to implement to honor God and man? Steven Covey, author of the now famous *7 Habits of Highly Effective People*, said, "The main thing is to keep the main thing the main thing."[2] So what's the main thing for Christians in faithfully navigating cyberspace with integrity? How do we start on this journey to surf our values? Just as important—how can we keep it going?

Seven Habits of Online Integrity

I'd like to offer you seven habits to faithfully navigate the brave new Web, which will hopefully become regular practices in your life. One goal of this list is to establish a basic framework for individuals to surf their values. I call these seven habits, because once implemented, we can continue to grow and mature in each area with a firm foundation. These are action-oriented disciplines that strive to be "non-techie," easy to understand, and flexible to implement based upon need. See table 7 for a quick outline.

Initially, I recommend applying these in order, but many readers will find that they are already further along in one or more areas.

In the next chapter we'll discuss habits four through seven in detail. In this chapter I want to concentrate on the first three habits. These three habits provide an essential foundation for surfing

Habit #1	Refresh Your Values in Cyberspace
Habit #2	Pledge Personal Online Integrity
Habit #3	Seek Trusted Accountability
Habit #4	Apply Helpful Technology
Habit #5	Balance Online and Offline Life
Habit #6	Practice Humble Authenticity
Habit #7	Become a Cyber Ambassador for Good

Table 7. Seven Habits of Online Integrity

your values. You may be tempted to jump straight to habit four and start applying technology without a genuine understanding of what problems you are trying to fix. Just as a builder of a house develops clear plans before pouring the foundation, we need to lay rock-solid principles that will withstand the inevitable virtual storms.

You'll see that a major theme behind all seven habits is to improve communication with those you trust and respect. Fighting this battle alone will lead to failure. On the contrary, through prayer, by working with God-given family relationships, by working within a fellowship of believers, and by working with reliable friends, coworkers, and industry partners, personal online risks can be dramatically reduced. This won't be easy, but as Confucius said, "A journey of a thousand miles begins with a single step." Most importantly, positive virtues— rather than a focus on the negatives—will be emphasized and encouraged to enable virtual integrity that will endure over the long term.

Habit #1: Refresh Your Values in Cyberspace

Everyone has a worldview. "A worldview provides a model of the world which guides its adherents in the world."[3] Our worldview can be determined by answering questions like: How do you explain human nature? What happens to a person at death? How do you determine what is right and wrong?[4] The answers to these worldview questions will guide your values and direct your life. (For example, The Family Research Council and Focus on the Family created a website to help Christians vote their values.[5])

To redeem our cyberspace, each of us needs to clarify some basic questions and answers about life (our worldview) and apply that worldview to our actions in cyberspace. Renewing your values in cyberspace requires three basic steps:

1. Reexamine offline (or "real-world") values/beliefs based upon the Bible.
2. Compare and contrast online and offline thoughts and behaviors.
3. (Re)Establish a list of values and behaviors for online life.

Step 1. Reexamine Offline Values

Our first task is to reexamine our beliefs and values regarding offline or "real" life. What do you believe? What actions are appropriate and encouraged, and what actions are inappropriate or wrong? Our pastors, churches, family, and friends should certainly help us here. At the simplest level, write down two lists—an "encourage or do" list and a "discourage or don't do" list.

What the Earliest Christians Did and Encouraged	What the Earliest Christians Did Not Do and Discouraged
Compassion	Adultery
Honesty	Anger
Humility	Greed
Marriage sanctity	Hypocrisy
Justice	Idolatry
Mercy	Immorality
Morality and ethics	Lustful looking
Overcoming evil with good	Materialism
Prayer for all, including enemies	Prejudice
Generosity	Intoxication

Table 8. Sample List of Earliest Christian Values and Practices[6]

The critical importance of understanding and incorporating Christian values as a part of technology training was identified over a decade ago by the Institute for Christian Teaching of Seventh-day Adventists. Their strategy paper defines important terms and identifies the relevance to all areas of life. "Ethics, particularly Christian ethics, should be viewed as vital to the technology program in Adventist schools, as our desire is to educate students for life and service in this world as well as for occupancy in the world to come."[7]

There are many helpful websites that can aid you in examining your values. BibleTexts.com lists the values of the earliest Christians as well as their practices.[8] Scripture references and other historical details regarding each value are available at their website. Of course, there are different opinions regarding Christian values, and table 8 is just a small subset of the BibleTexts.com list. Nevertheless, this list provides a good starting point to get the conversation going. It is also fair to say that all Christians support the moral guidance provided by the Ten Commandments and Christ's teaching in the Sermon on the Mount.

Each person must be comfortable with where they stand regarding "Christian ethics." My main purpose in this point is not to question different Christian values and beliefs, as long as they are biblically based. Rather, I urge you to inform and transform your online life by first clarifying overall values. I do strongly encourage discussion with others to facilitate this process.

Step 2. Compare and Contrast Values

Once you are comfortable with your values, you are ready to compare and contrast your online and offline values and behaviors. The end result of this step is a clear understanding of where your Christian worldview is clashing with your cyber values and behaviors. If you've come this far in this book, you should have a fairly good understanding of the kinds of problematic behaviors that are being renamed and encouraged in cyberspace. Take an honest assessment of your online life by writing down what you're doing and not doing. This list should contain the good, the bad, and the ugly.

Now the hard part. There are many ways to face this list, but self-examination is never easy. No doubt, there will be some embarrassing items on the list that you may feel uncomfortable sharing with others. While I strongly encourage an open and honest conversation with a trusted friend or spouse, you may not feel comfortable with sharing "cyber sins" at this point. The most important action is sincere repentance of wrongdoing before God. It's important to remember that this should not be just a list of the bad things but should also include positive things you're doing and not doing.

The Seventh-day Adventists developed a helpful online curriculum framework in business to assist adults in identifying values, clarifying values, making judgments, and making choices. This guide can help adults "show an appreciation of Christian principles such as honesty and integrity in all business transactions."[9] Guides like this one can facilitate discussion, with probing questions that identify underlying beliefs and values.

If you are having difficulty identifying differences between online and offline values, look at your online actions. What are you doing and not doing in cyberspace? How are you behaving on the computers at work? Are you saying the same things in real life that you're blogging in cyberspace? Where is integrity falling short? Go back and examine table 6 and see if you can relate to any of these behaviors.

One other consideration: After consistently behaving in certain ways, it is natural to become blind to wrongdoing and often rename activities or gradually change your definitions of right and wrong to match your behavior. Confiding in a friend who is behaving in the same manner may not identify these blind spots in your life. Talking with an older and wiser mentor can help. I also recommend working with someone of the same sex, if possible.

Step 3. (Re)Establish a List of Values and Behaviors for Online Life

The last step for refreshing your values in cyberspace is equivalent to "walking the talk" or "putting your money where your mouth is" in online life. The outcome of this step is a list of online values and behaviors that you will commit to implementing. The goal is to restore or refresh the link between your faith, your overall worldview, your list of online values, and specific Internet behaviors. While our worldview should not change between on-line and offline life, if you feel that certain activities are accept-able online that are taboo in offline life, discuss those areas of difference with your Christian friends. Don't focus only on the negative areas, but examine the exciting possibilities—positive areas where online integrity is being demonstrated. Build on those strengths.

One positive example is going back to school. Perhaps the Inter-net is helping you with career goals and taking classes online. You are dedicating yourself to positive development and learning more skills. You may be exploring a different career. In our fast-paced technological world, our knowledge quickly becomes outdated. Just when you've mastered MySpace, along comes Facebook. So we always have to keep learning. In this way, your offline value of lifetime learning and career growth is being enhanced and aided by the Internet.

An example of a conflict area might be the way that you are deceiving people online. You may not be truthful on social net-working sites. Or perhaps your instant messaging language is in-appropriate. You would never talk that way at church or in your home, but online you go to sites and say things that you know are not honoring God.

One caution regarding values and behaviors: I've seen many parents and teachers "impose" their values on their children and students with checklists of dos and don'ts. Too often, these lists are quickly discarded, violated, even mocked, since the individual rebels against imposed values. The goal of this first habit is for individuals to understand and determine their own values based upon their beliefs. While families, businesses, and schools need to issue "top-down" rules for others, the aim here is to encourage "bottom-up" buy-in. If pledges of integrity and accountability (habits 2 and 3) are not working, it may be that the original values were merely imposed and not authentically owned.

Once you have written down and discussed your online values and behaviors, I urge you to condense the list to the top two or three behaviors that you want to encourage in your life, and a few (no more than five) behaviors that you want to eliminate or reduce. Try to be specific about actions, but not so specific that you need a new list for every website you visit. Again, discuss this list with trusted friends, family members, or your mentor. This list is crucial as we move to habits 2 and 3.

If you are addicted to inappropriate Internet activities, these three steps probably won't adequately address your weaknesses. Get help. You can start with your pastor or find a good Christian counseling center. I urge you to take action before addictions take on an even larger role in your life.

Habit #2: Pledge Personal Online Integrity

Once you've assessed your values and online behaviors, you are ready to make a cyber pledge of integrity. An initial commitment to integrity is essential to every other step in this process. By stating our intentions, a wide variety of supporting structures (people, processes, and technology) can be put in place to assist us in surfing our values.

Most Americans make one or more New Year's resolutions every year: lose weight, take a class, stop smoking, get in shape, learn the piano, or a myriad of other plans to better themselves. We ask our friends and family to help us keep these new commitments. Making this pledge is similar to, but much more important than, committing to a diet or exercise program.

Just as we need to dedicate ourselves to exercise and diet programs to remain physically healthy, we need to intentionally act to live out our online faith. Others can't do it for us. Each person must first set clear goals. Since many of us have slipped in our diets or exercise regimens, this analogy may not sit well with you, but the point is that you need a plan.

Making a pledge places a mark at a memorable moment in time. Our culture values public statements of belief. When the going gets tough, we remember those. For many, a public commitment provides the added incentive and needed specifics to persevere over time and when principles face testing. It also provides a public signal to friends and family that they can challenge you to keep your word. We all need help and accountability.

Name it what you like: cyber values, surfing resolution, family online contract, opting in to integrity, or a virtual commitment. This is your personal Internet mission statement that articulates your desire to align your online life with the values you profess. Your statement doesn't need to be a public pronouncement on MySpace or Facebook (although it could be). However, at a minimum, your pledge will be shared with some of your closest friends and family.

I'll soon lay out more specific steps that will help you create your personal "online manifesto" or adopt one of the many that have already been created by others. But first, I'd like to address a few questions related to this commitment. Why is a pledge for my virtual life so important? Is this just a negative list of "censored sites," such as porn, that I can't visit? No—it's much more than that. Here's why.

The Need: A Positive Vision for Virtual Life

Pledges, resolutions, and professed commitments have been made since the beginning of time. They seal your promises in a special way. If genuinely coming from the heart and not forced, they express a deep desire to commit to a mission. While some mock them, most take them very seriously, even dying for a cause after making a pledge of loyalty.

Many Christians profess their beliefs every week at church in the words of the Apostles' Creed or Nicene Creed. Children pledge allegiance to their country's flag at school. These are positive pledges and statements of belief. They may also have implications for what you don't believe. For example, Christians use these creeds to affirm the doctrine of the Trinity. Other religions believe in God but not the Trinity. But to recite the Nicene Creed as a pledge is first and foremost to commit to a faith in the Trinitarian God. Likewise, if you pledge allegiance to the United States of America, you are implicitly placing your homeland above other countries.

In the same way, a cyber pledge should not just be a list of online behaviors you don't support.

Throughout the Bible, many men and women pray for grace to honor commitments made to God and man. King David wrote these words: "I will set before my eyes no vile thing."[10] But he also wrote hundreds of positive statements about what he will do with his life. Consider, for example, "I will extol the LORD at all times; his praise will always be on my lips. . . . Turn from evil and do good; seek peace and pursue it."[11] His love for God is represented in positive ways much more than in lists of what he won't be doing.

Similarly, our online commitment should be mainly a positive statement. One leader once said it like this: "If you spend your time doing the dos, you won't have time to do the don'ts."[12] Just as children discipline themselves to play the piano so that later in life they can be creative and make beautiful music, online discipline reaps rewards in later life. Or, think of marriage vows, which are primarily a positive statement of commitment. While it is true and important that couples add the lines, "forsaking all others," the overall focus to the ceremony is always a positive one.

Defining Your Cyber Pledge, From Kids to Adults

So, exactly what might a pledge of integrity in the virtual world look like? An online search for Internet pledges of integrity will yield plenty of excellent examples. From companies doing business online to family Internet contracts to cyber commitments for pastors and individuals, there are many excellent resources available. I'll consider some of the most popular ones first.

Following is an abbreviated version of a Family Internet Safety Pledge[13] from www.Safefamilies.org. It's clearly oriented toward youth:

1. I will not look at, download, or copy inappropriate or questionable material.
2. I will not give any personal information.
3. I will not arrange to meet anyone in person that I find out about online.

4. I will always be courteous in how I communicate to others.

5. I will not purchase products or services online without my parents' approval and help.

6. I will not respond to email or an instant message from someone I do not know.

7. I will follow my parents' or guardians' guidelines for when I can use the computer.

8. I will not install software programs without getting permission. I understand that peer-to-peer file sharing programs like Kazaa, Limewire, or BearShare are not allowed.

9. I will not use the computer to do anything illegal, including illegal downloading of software, music, or movies.

10. These rules apply wherever I am (at home, a friend's house, school, or the library).

11. I understand that violating this pledge may result in loss of computer access, and I will accept these consequences.

For another example focused on a family pledge, *USA Today*'s technology section reported that Microsoft and the national Parent-Teacher Association (PTA) urge parents to make a "PACT" to help determine what types of media are appropriate.

> The "P" stands for parental involvement. The "A" is for determining what your child can access online. "C" is picking the content you deem OK for little ones. And "T" stands for time, as in when and how long the kids can play. . . . The Entertainment Software Rating Board tries to guide parents. But their ratings don't give the full story. WhatTheyPlay.com is a new website that helps parents understand how ratings apply to the titles their kids want to play.[14]

Other helpful sites for family pledges include www.safekids.com/contract_kid.htm and www.protectkids.com/parentsafety/pledge.htm. For crafting pledges of children of various ages, I like www.netsmartz.org/resources/pledge.htm.

For an example of a virtual integrity workplace pledge, consider that offered by the International Council of Online Professionals, which declares that Honesty + Accountability + Integrity = Excellence.[15]

For churches, the First Baptist Church of Troy, Michigan, has a nice website with helpful guidance: www.fbctroy.org/church/internet.htm; pastors can gain some excellent cyber guidance at: www.safefamilies.org/docs/manual_pastors.doc. This site offers an "Online Safety and Media Sobriety Manual for Pastors," which covers the following topics in detail:

1. Commitment to Media Sobriety
2. Commitment to Protect Children Online
3. Commitment to Protect Children from All Second-Hand Smut
4. Commitment to Get Educated on Online and Media Safety
5. Commitment to Appropriate Communication
6. Commitment to Avoid Online Affairs
7. Commitment to Recovery: to enter recovery and sign the Media Sobriety Covenant for Adults in Recovery if I am not able to maintain these commitments and maintain media sobriety.
8. Commitment to Supporting Others in Recovery

A Shorter Pledge for Adults

While I think that explicit instructions and agreements are needed for children, I believe shorter, simpler pledges are more powerful for adults. Far from being watered-down, fewer words can be more encompassing when coming from one who freely commits himself or herself based upon biblically based convictions and obedience. Consider David's words one more time, this time as a possible pledge of virtual integrity: "I will set before my eyes no vile thing."[16] Many pages, even books, full of prohibited items can't come close to the power of those nine words.

That simple resolution from King David has endured for over three thousand years. Yes, this is the same David who violated his own pledge, and he paid dearly for that mistake. It is often those who have made mistakes that have learned the importance of discipline.

Whatever your views on history, the Bible, or David himself, this model provides a powerfully moral way to surf the net.

Other versions of this passage use the words *worthless* or *wicked* instead of *vile*. However, the word *vile* captures both concepts. If you look up *vile* in a thesaurus, you'll see words like *evil, despicable, depraved, contemptible, base, degraded, loathsome, foul, disgusting*, and *horrible*. The original Latin word captures the concept of *cheap*.

Stated a few other ways, I won't cheapen myself or waste my time accessing material that I know is evil and can cause problems that would violate my integrity. I won't intentionally surf the Internet to access content that I know is wrong. By making this pledge, you recognize that this material is bad for you and will eventually lead to harm. Just as smoking one cigarette after another can cause cancer, I make myself susceptible to moral and spiritual cancer by engaging my mind in inappropriate surfing, downloading, chatting, or any "vile" behavior. This pledge recognizes that it all starts with the individual thoughts.

So who decides what qualifies as vile online? Answer: you do, hopefully with a well-informed conscience and your accountability partner(s). While I do think there are plenty of black-and-white examples I might give, the gray area is so much larger. There isn't one simple answer to this question, but there are plenty of places you can go for advice and direction. By the way, I call this your "integrity line." It's the boundary you won't cross to view what's vile.

Some may not feel ready to take David's pledge. If you are one of them, perhaps you can commit to a simpler pledge. Say these words to your spouse, a trusted friend, colleague, or family member: "I will surf with integrity." By taking this step, you reaffirm your convictions to those you love. You declare that you will take specific actions to do what you say and say what you'll do in cyberspace.

As we've seen, for the pledge to be successful it needs to come from the heart. If you resent this pledge or if you secretly grumble and complain that it's totally unreasonable, the pledge will have an opposite effect on you. Like a dieter with a constant craving for chocolate cake, you'll go online and find yourself looking for dubious content.

Don't get me wrong. Making this pledge sincerely won't take away the temptations. The apostle Peter was sincere but still betrayed Jesus. So we will certainly slip and sin at some point. But the important question is where your heart is when initially pledging integrity with a spouse, parent, or coworker. As Father Ronald Rolheiser writes, "While sincerity doesn't necessarily save us from sin, it does help us hear the rooster crow. As long as we remain sincere, we will soon enough admit our sin and we will know too that God still looks on us with love, even in betrayal."[17]

Reservations: I Already Follow Policies at Work

Perhaps you are already a model cyber citizen and follow policies at school, work, and home. Another pledge may seem like another speed limit, one that's unnecessary. And yet this is really a question of the heart. Are you just following mandatory procedures, or are you actively engaged in surfing your values?

Let me be clear on one point. Acceptable use policies at businesses need to be very detailed for legal reasons. In addition, many staff sign off on rules they have no intention of following. Oftentimes, the only thing motivating compliance is the fear of getting caught and being disciplined. These lists of dos and don'ts enable the "cyber police" to formally discipline employees who violate policies. But there is no work policy anywhere in the world as powerful as David's words, when offered with a sincere heart.

Many people disagree with their school's, library's, or company's acceptable use policies, but they still follow the rules. In my experience, employees who disagree with Internet policies often become the first violators of those same policies. These staff members go around filters and engage in behaviors that make life difficult for the cyber police and get themselves in trouble.

Still, most employees sign those acceptable use policies as a condition of employment. For better or for worse, they agree up front, even if their heart isn't in it. They make an initial pledge to follow certain rules of conduct, even if those policies are forced. These half-hearted commitments leave people open to online attacks. As I've noted, surveys show that most inappropriate online activity occurs during work hours. Bottom line: taking this pledge will help protect you at both home and work, since this simple pledge goes well beyond corporate policies.

Habit #3: Seek Trusted Accountability

Twenty-first-century Americans are notoriously independent people. We like to keep things to ourselves and show only our best face in public. While women are, in general, much better at sharing personal thoughts with friends than are men, the extended family support system that existed in this country for centuries has all but disappeared.[18] No doubt, the Internet has enabled new global communities of mutual hobbies and interests, such as fantasy football or multiplayer games. However, these groups tend to form for convenience, and they lack the trust, personal accountability, and moral direction that extended families offered men and women even a generation ago.

Even churchgoing Christians are becoming more independent. More and more people try to slip in and out of church services without being noticed. Many have a "personal religion" at home or consider a TV or Internet ministry as their community of believers, if they have one at all. We are wary of others' direction in our personal lives.

Hiding under popular banners like leisure, freedom, even "private faith," most people flee from accountability in their personal lives—especially when it comes to their online activity. We're just too busy, too private, too proud, too liberated, or too self-supporting to be bothered. But are we being foolish or too shortsighted to recognize what could help us address our weaknesses?

The hard-won wisdom of the business world would suggest we are. Successful businesses understand accountability. Not only does Wall Street have a myriad of financial expectations that affect a company's stock price, customers demand service-level agreements. Even if your company is privately held or a nonprofit or government organization, auditors hold you accountable based on predetermined guidelines that determine if the integrity of the organization is being upheld.

On a personal level, most staff have an employee performance appraisal that evaluates your results from a variety of perspectives.

In our new global competitive environment, where jobs are being outsourced to India and China, every aspect of a person's productivity is analyzed, from sick leave used to product delivery. The bottom line is that most of us are held accountable for delivering projects on time and on budget at work—and rightfully so.

Consider the Project Management Institute (PMI),[19] a global nonprofit organization of more than 240,000 professionals in over 160 countries, with their Project Management Body of Knowledge (PMBOK). These pragmatic processes have become the combined wisdom that enables projects to succeed. Training and certification programs help professionals become certified by PMI. If team members question why a certain approach is needed or why they are being held responsible, some aspect of the PMBOK is quoted, because these principles have been proven to work.

How important is accountability to PMI experts?

> Only when all team members—including project managers and project sponsors—understand their role and what they are accountable and responsible for achieving will projects accomplish results close to the outcome expected.[20]

Many books, articles, and best-practice guides highlight the importance of clearly delineating project responsibilities, individual acceptance of these responsibilities, and each team member's willingness to be accountable for the activities assigned to them. One popular website said that the habit that bosses love most is accountability by staff.[21]

In short, if discipline and accountability make sense at the office, they may make sense at home.

Models That Work

There is another area where accountability has been shown to make a major difference. Consider for a moment the disciplines around diet and fitness.

New diets are announced all the time, and there is no shortage of advice on this popular topic. In fact, "expert advice" often changes and contradicts other wisdom. One website in the United Kingdom has declared, "the failure of the one size fits all diet. . . . This attitude does not treat us as an individual and as a result will fail the vast majority of the people it is intended to help."[22]

So what is the key? Doctors and scientists have found that accountability is just as important as choosing the right regimen. One program that has excelled for over forty-five years is Weight Watchers. Why is it successful? With over 1.5 million members around the world, Weight Watchers motivates and provides information at regular meetings where dieters join others in practice: "Affirming your commitment to yourself." What does that entail? "Once you've decided to lose weight, holding yourself accountable is essential to achieving success. That's the purpose of the meeting's private weigh-in. Our members find that meetings and private weigh-ins help them keep their resolve and motivation."[23] A recent study published in the *Journal of the American Medical Association* found that people who had followed the Weight Watchers Points program for two years lost an average of about six pounds. Those who also attended Weight Watchers meetings were found to be more successful, losing an average of eleven pounds after two years.[24]

Virtual Integrity Watchers = The Right Cyber Diet

Just as Weight Watchers helps members measure progress in their health, we each need "virtual integrity watchers" in our lives to help us stay accountable to the commitments we make to ourselves, to others, and to God. Accountability partners should provide encouragement and support our efforts.

So how can we establish an online approach for the long-term that is sensible for busy lifestyles? Once you are comfortable with a pledge of online integrity, the next step is to seek accountability. If you've been working with others that you trust up to this point, those individuals may be best positioned to understand your values and help you implement your online pledge.

On the other hand, some people prefer to establish a separate group of same-sex Christian friends whom they can count on to hold them accountable. The key is being accountable to one or more people that you trust, and with whom you can openly discuss life and where you draw lines. This is very hard at first but gets easier over time. You should pick someone who is committed to you and has your best interests in mind. For married couples, your spouse is an important first person, but you may also want to include another person of the same sex, such as a brother, sister, or respected friend.

For example, my wife and I talk about our worldview, and she knows my online and offline values. We've even agreed on parameters for our family "vile" line. And yet, I also get together with a group of businessmen on a regular basis for breakfast to hold me accountable for my online and offline actions.

There's a trap to avoid here. Don't be accountable to someone you know will be too easy on you or someone who has immoral intentions. Just as a coach who says you don't need to practice doesn't really have your best interest in mind, so a friend who is actually tempting you with more vile content should not be your choice.

There are also many men's and women's accountability groups established at churches to help in these areas. If you don't have these types of programs at your church, perhaps you can start a group. Several national programs, like Promise Keepers, also offer accountability groups with their own set of cyber promises and conferences to motivate and train men. There are also several Christian women's groups, like Proverbs 31 Ministries, that can help the ladies find support with integrity in their online and offline lives.[25]

Accountability: What Do We Talk About?

I encourage accountability partners/groups to discuss all aspects of virtual integrity. It can be done in fun ways. In fact, I discourage just going through the negative aspects of surfing. Just as food falls into different categories, so do websites and online activities. For example, here is one way of thinking about categories to discuss:

1. Helpful or required activities: Christian websites, online schools, professional training, work-related activities, online Bible studies, cool new things to do.
2. Gray areas: sports, news, dating sites, eBay, online trading, chatting, traveling sites, IM with friends.
3. Sins: lust, lying, cheating, stealing, etc.

And yet, there are not right or wrong ways to go about a conversation with trusted friends. The more open and transparent the discussion, the better. Proverbs 27:17 says, "As iron sharpens iron/ So a man sharpens the countenance of his friend" (NKJV).

Most of all, we need to remember that our ultimate accountability is to God. I love this quote from D. Martyn Lloyd-Jones:

Say this every day to revolutionize your life: "Throughout the whole of this day, everything I do, and say, and attempt, and think, and imagine, is going to be done under the eye of God. He is going to be with me; He sees everything; He knows everything. There is nothing I can do or attempt but God is fully aware of it all."[26]

8 ➡ Surf Your Values

More Habits to Keep Integrity Going

Simplicity is the ultimate sophistication.

Leonardo da Vinci (1452–1519)[1]

"Keep it simple." That was the clear message I heard over and over again from computer users back in the year 2000. We were redesigning our Michigan Information Technology Services Division (ITSD) website, and our talented and enthusiastic Web development team had visions of bells and whistles—and complexity. We had just successfully navigated the "Y2K" (Year 2000) computer bug, and the new possibilities with technology seemed endless.

But our Department of Management and Budget customer interviews brought us back to reality. "Answer the basic questions with fewer clicks" was our real challenge. "Get rid of complicated acronyms and hard-to-find content. Drop the organizational charts and give us helpful information we need now." So we changed course and ended up with a customer-focused website that was centered on simple themes like: "My PC, My Consultant, My Connection."[2] Today, as we transition into another new generation of amazing technology, a central goal must be clear-cut answers that work simply.

Steve Jobs, CEO of Apple Computer, said this at a user conference: "I know you have 1,000 great ideas for things that iTunes *could* do. And we have 1,000 more. But innovation is not about saying 'yes' to everything. It's about saying 'no' to all but the most crucial features."[3]

So how can we apply technology in easy-to-use ways that help individuals and families navigate virtual complexity with integrity? Once you have reaffirmed your values, made a pledge of online integrity, and selected an accountability partner (or partners), you are ready to reexamine technology that can help. On the other hand, if accountability software is imposed on you or others without a sincere pledge of integrity, the technology we will discuss will be viewed not only as a hindrance but possibly even as "spyware which monitors behavior and should be removed."[4]

I am limiting the scope of my discussion of habit 4 to identity theft (including Internet safety) and integrity theft (including cyber ethics), as defined earlier in the book. This approach is far from an exhaustive look at the topic but does provide a framework that attempts to keep technology simple and yet establish helpful personal habits.

Habit #4: Apply Helpful Technology

Applying helpful technology entails five "life-cycle" steps.

Step 1. Education and research on Net and TV access devices
Step 2. Making product selection(s) based on your specific needs
Step 3. Installing and configuring products
Step 4. Maintaining the technology
Step 5. Reexamination of network, ongoing training, returning to Step 1

These steps may seem daunting to some, but just as with following a diet or an exercise program, plenty of excellent help is available all the way through the process. Some may immediately say that this is just too hard and insist on the need to rely on an ISP or a company service like Best Buy's "Geek Squad."[5] But be careful. Just as in any business, you can outsource the technology or service but not the responsibility or risk. The key to success is consistency.

Although most people will already have some level of software or internet service provider security and/or filtering service already in place, I urge you to reexamine your needs for a complete solution. During the first two steps of this process, start thinking about what technology should stay and what needs to be added or replaced.

Step 1. Education and Research

It would be great if one software package or service provided Internet protection that would not only stop viruses and online fraud, but also scan all of our virtual activities to match personalized values and flag risks to professed beliefs. I hope to see technology like that someday. But currently technology tools to help in surfing your values come in at least three different broad categories: (1) computer security (including antivirus software, personal firewall, spyware removal, etc.), (2) Web filtering software (sometimes called parental controls), and (3) accountability software. The computer industry and most home computer owners recognize the first two categories, but the majority of Americans have never been introduced to accountability software. The good news is that there are plenty of excellent Web resources available to help us stay current.

See table 9 for a list of free Web-based educational recommendations to get you started. Whether you are new to the Web or an Internet expert, I highly recommend taking some time to visit a few of these resources. New technology and new ideas are always coming onto the scene. Staying informed on technology trends is an important first step—even if you're afraid of your TV remote control.

There is so much excellent training available on these portals that no summary will do justice to the benefits they provide. If you are looking for a single recommendation for the security actions that need to be taken at home, I recommend the "Seven Steps to Safer Computing from FTC."[6] If you are looking for a summary

Name/ Web Address (URL)	Sample Content/Benefits
Safe Families www.safefamilies.org	Web tutorials, safety news, free software, resources for parents, pastors, nonprofits, software
Learn The Net.com www.learnthenet.com	Great "how to" guide on everything dotcom, free courses, quizzes, games
Get with It (from Ireland) A Parent's Guide to New Media Technologies www.iab.ie/Publications/Get_With_It_low_res1.pdf	Great starter reference guide to answer basic questions. Points to answers internationally.
Stop, Think, Click www.OnGuardOnline.gov	Seven Steps to Safer Computing from FTC, security startup tips
The Webwise Online Course www.bbc.co.uk/webwise/course/	Learn how to use the Internet, step by step. Links to additional free materials
Cyber Angels www.cyberangels.org	Helpful guides, multimedia presentations, help lines, and training on staying safe
The TV Boss www.TheTVboss.org	Helpful guide to using parental controls for television
Internet Safety Coalition www.ikeepsafe.org	FAQs, Faux Paw books for kids, Parents Resource Center, video clips
National Cyber Security Alliance www.staysafeonline.org	Top 8 Cyber Security Practices, answers for: home, small business, K–12, and higher ed, free PC check

Table 9. Trusted Web Training

description of software tools for the second two categories (Web filtering and accountability), I would visit Safe Families.[7]

I also mention the Cyber Angels website, which includes a list of computer and cyberspace-related acronyms that parents should know, as well as helpful advice, such as avoiding provocative names that draw attention and send the wrong messages online. If you're looking for a helpful booklet that explains computer terms and acronyms, the Irish guide entitled, *Get with It: A Parent's Guide to New Media Technologies,* is worth downloading and printing out. All of these sites contain links to other helpful information as well. The best thing about this online content is that it is constantly updated for accuracy and current relevance.

While there's much more excellent technical training and advice on the Web, watch out for sites that try to sell you a specific product in the process. When researching personal solutions, use unbiased analyses such as the annual product comparisons by *PC Magazine.*[8] If you're looking for security product recommendations for businesses, I recommend visiting *SC Magazine.*[9]

On the other hand, once you have narrowed your software choices to just a few options, vendor websites like Microsoft.com and Symantec.com can provide a wealth of excellent guidance and more details on specific product functionality for home or business. Since most people buy computer products and install them with all of the default settings, take this opportunity to go back and learn more about the products and services that you already use.

Don't forget to research solutions for each "input device" that you use for the Internet. There is no doubt that "tempting the click" covers more than PCs. New attacks and new defenses are occurring daily, so you need to be aware of all "doors into cyberspace." A big weakness for many people is their cell phones or other portable Internet-access devices. The merger of Internet and TV is another area that requires additional research for your particular situation. I recommend going to the website for the products that you own to learn what capabilities already exist for family protection.

Step 2. Making Product Selection(s) Based on Your Specific Needs

As you wrap up your research, here are a few things to keep in mind when choosing software packages or managed Internet safety solutions:

A. Don't believe everything that's written on the box or website. While technical advice is usually trustworthy, broad promises from technology companies, like "Use the Internet free from temptation," are overblown and nothing more than marketing hype.

B. Look for independent verification of functionality, or better yet, a personal recommendation from a trusted friend who uses the product.

C. Look for a good company track record and a stable product. Be wary of brand new products and companies. While industry consolidation is commonplace and some excellent companies change their names when bought, look for a track record of success with products that are on at least the second or third release (versions 2.1 and higher).

D. Free is good, but it isn't always the right choice. There are many free offers, but make sure you know whom you're dealing with. Is the company reputable? Is the software updated regularly? Can you call for help (on weekends too)?

As the FTC outlines, the minimum two steps that everyone should take for their personal computers are:

- Use anti-virus and anti-spyware software, as well as a firewall, and update them all regularly.
- Make sure your operating system and Web browser are set up properly, and update them regularly.[10]

Several companies, like McAfee and Symantec (Norton), offer bundled security packages that combine a wide range of security functions in one solution. For example, Norton Internet Security offers: Spyware protection, Antivirus, Two-Way Firewall, Advanced Phishing Protection, Intrusion Prevention, and Rootkit Detection.[11] (In February 2008, Antispam and Parental Controls were available add-on packs for Norton Internet Security.)

In general, most families understand the importance of antivirus (AV) software, because they can go to their local computer electronics store, or even Wal-Mart, and easily purchase this software. Many people buy this Internet protection as a package deal with their tax preparation software in the January–April timeframe each year. In addition, AV initially comes free with most computers, and the AV vendors will prompt you to renew your subscription automatically—typically after a year.

If you have a more advanced network set up at home with high-speed Internet (broadband) and multiple computers that are networked together, you will probably want to choose an Internet filtering router with commercial filtering, rather than software on each computer, especially if you don't have filtered Internet service from your ISP. The benefit of this approach is that every computer will have the same level of protection, and you have to configure things only once. Typically, this setup is also more difficult to bypass than separate software for each PC.

Accountability: New Software Options

Pick up just about any recent book on home networks, and you will read advice similar to the actions discussed so far in this section on Internet security and filtering. But the majority of readers will be unfamiliar with accountability software options. What is accountability software? Put simply, this software sends a report of all your Internet activities to your trusted accountability partner(s) to check up and provide metrics on.

If this software is used by choice and not force, it can provide a powerful disincentive to viewing unacceptable material and surfing your values. Since there are many circumvention technologies available, this approach can end the natural tendencies to get around filters. It is generally intended to supplement, not replace, filtering software, but it can help reduce temptations for a dad or mom who, as the systems administrator for the family Web filter, can go around protections. While it was initially a separate category of software, companies like SafeEyes[12] are now bundling accountability with filtering software, but they are still calling it "parental control" software. We need to think about adult accountability too.

The first accountability software company was Covenant Eyes,[13] and there are now many other competing products, like X3Watch Pro[14] and Eye Promise,[15] on the market. There are also many free accountability software downloads (which I discourage); they typically have less functionality and no technical support.

Here's a short description of Covenant Eyes product functionality in January 2008:

- Monitors all websites, newsgroups, and most file sharing sites visited on your computer
- Reports are always stored so they cannot be erased
- Multiple users on one account have their own separate records

- Multiple users on one account can have their own account-ability partners
- Scores every website even if it is a brand new website that has never been reviewed by filter programs
- Unlimited number of accountability partners at no extra charge
- Unlimited number of computers—add to other computers at no extra charge
- Accountability partners access your report at no charge to them
- You can choose to selectively block protocols, like file sharing programs
- Works with all computers and Internet connections
- Protection against circumvention
- Easy-to-read reports[16]

While many churches and other Christian organizations use accountability software, it is rarely found in businesses and homes today. Most large organizations, like the State of Michigan, use a good enterprise-wide filtering product like Websense. The fifteen or so categories that are blocked, such as spyware and porn (out of more than seventy categories), are decided on by a group of senior business executives, but they are not tailored to individuals, due to the administrative overhead and the flexibility that business areas desire.

Michigan government has two people administering Websense software for about 55,000 employees. While this approach is very efficient and meets legal and security requirements, it lacks the necessary breadth and depth required as we enter into the second decade of the twenty-first century. I'm referring to the myriad of unique situations coming at us from sites like Facebook, YouTube, MySpace, and others.

But the biggest reason that I support peer accountability on a massive scale is that it eliminates the "defeat the cyber police" mentality at work. Quite simply, it allows employees to personalize their Web experience (bottom-up) for integrity and accountability. For those who choose not to have accountability partners, they would still meet the basic acceptable use agreement regulations and be monitored by the (friendly) "cyber police."

Some may be thinking, You're the CISO—just make it happen. Unfortunately, the functionality I describe is not in place today with enterprise Web products to allow this model to work. Yes, you can still have personal accountability at work with a coworker, but cultural and technology issues need to be addressed prior to rolling out software in most workplaces. I expect more such software will be developed and installed by companies. As problems grow, the demand for new answers for business areas will become a scream.

Far from disabling or discouraging the Internet, accountability enables much to happen. This software builds trust and allows the use of Internet tools that must currently be banned because of the abuses that are possible by the minority. For example, many businesses ban social networking sites or watching video clips due to the inability to segment traffic into good and bad. This policy tempts some employees to go around security protections to get the content anyway.

For the same reasons, many families ban all Google images or photo sites due to the porn pictures. The sad part is that many "good" pictures are missed, and we throw the cyber baby out with the bathwater. Just as wearing car seatbelts does not imply that the driver is unsafe and reckless, applying accountability software need not imply that every user surfs without integrity. This software will assist in such issues as telework (work from home). With the Internet changing so fast, personal accountability with metrics must be a priority to enable new innovation.

Other Temptation-Blocking Software

I have listed three main categories of software services that will help you surf your values, but there are certainly other software products that can be used to help fight an assortment of other temptations. One example is the (free) "Temptation Blocker," which aids personal discipline by using reminders and timers to help you focus on one task at a time. (It was originally developed to help the author stop playing the game Half Life 2 when he had deadlines to meet.) Here's a description of the free software available at http://thenetreporter.com/temptation-blocker.html:

Once the software installs, you start it up and see a list of the programs in your computer's Start Menu. You can check off the ones
you want to block, tell it how long to block them, and then get to
work. If you ever give in to temptation and try to start the blocked
programs, a dialogue box pops up telling you how much longer
until the programs are available again.[17]

One warning: software like this should not be loaded onto work
computers without complying with relevant policies and procedures.
My hope is to see these types of personal productivity tools, as well
as accountability software, built into future versions of enterprise-
wide filters from the leading security vendors.

The University of Michigan has launched a service that helps students avoid unintentionally infringing on copyrighted material. Called
"Be Aware You're Uploading" (BAYU), this system detects when students in residence halls upload files using peer-to-peer technology
to access content. An informational website contains school policies,
helpful advice, and practical steps if you receive an e-mail notification
from the BAYU system. Here's a sample from their website:[18]

You can:

1. Disable peer-to-peer file sharing applications on your system
   to reduce the likelihood that you will share copyrighted files
   or expose yourself to computer viruses or other unwanted
   access to your computer;
2. Completely remove peer-to-peer file sharing applications on
   your system to avoid the risks associated with peer-to-peer file
   sharing technology (there are numerous important and lawful
   applications, some of which are used routinely in academic and
   classroom settings, so this is not always possible or desirable).

Step 3. Installing and Configuring Products

Installing and configuring the software can be a daunting task.
While most software will load easily with helpful wizards, things can
get confusing if you customize your installation. For this reason,
many just go with the default settings (or keep hitting the "next"

button). While the intention may be to go back later and fine-tune the configuration to your needs, major changes are seldom made after initial setup. My point: try to get it right the first time by reading through the instructions (which may be on the product website) before the installation. Most reputable companies also have toll-free numbers that you can call for help.

The first important question in installation and configuration is this: Who will be the systems administrator? Or, in other words, who has the passwords to make changes, bypass filters, delete the logs, even turn off or change which websites are blocked? In most families, this usually becomes the parent who is the most technically qualified. While this makes for a smoother installation, be careful.

This is an area where many families and offices first get into trouble. While there is no easy answer here, talk about how you want things to work before you assign roles. Temptations will certainly come for the smartest technical person in the house or workplace, so honesty and transparency is essential in this discussion. One possible solution includes using accountability software that keeps track of all configuration changes and sends activity to trusted partners (in another family or work area). Another solution is using filtered Internet provided by your ISP or external provider. But no matter what choices you make, someone will likely be able to make changes, just as with parental controls on your TV. Talk through different situations to reduce temptations for Internet, TV, and cell phone access.

One problem that many home PC users run into is preventing anti-spyware software or other programs from overwriting or disabling your Web filtering software. While this is fairly easy to fix (by configuring your anti-spyware software to allow and not remove Web filtering or accountability software), watch out for members of the family or "helpful colleagues" at the office who use this excuse to disable Web filtering in the name of security. Once again, if all else fails, call your security vendor to get help.

Step 4. Maintaining the Technology

Once your software is configured and everything is working, a process is needed to keep the technology updated and working properly in the long-term. Unfortunately, many home users either don't understand the need to maintain a subscription to get regular updates or don't want to pay for it. Web filtering technologies, operating system software, and security tools require frequent updates to ensure that the latest threats are being blocked. These updates should happen automatically if the computers are configured properly. But consider this fact: "The latest in user security metrics shows that only five percent of surveyed systems were fully up to date, with all applications patched and running the latest versions."[19]

Some of the tasks associated with maintaining the technology include:

A. Updating subscriptions (usually annually) and paying bills for AV, security, accountability and other software. This may be bundled with paying Internet access bills.
B. Ensuring that the software is loaded and running properly on a regular basis. I recommend semi-annual check-ups, at a minimum, to ensure proper functioning.
C. Checking for alerts or other flagged items in the computer logs that are generated by many products or parental controls.
D. Running "clean-up" utilities that help the computer run faster and more efficiently, by such methods as deleting unneeded files. Many computers come with helpful utilities installed.

These tasks can often be done fairly quickly. Don't neglect them. Whether at home or at work, identifying clear responsibilities for computer maintenance for the short- and long-term are essential. I try to schedule maintenance activities at the same time that I back up important files and documents, or install new tax software, or make any other changes.

Step 5. Reexamination of Network, Ongoing Training, Returning to Step 1

This last step is a natural extension of step 4, but I break it out because it typically happens less frequently and involves new thinking and more people than simply maintaining your current technology.

This step can include important decisions like moving to high-speed Internet access,[20] which will likely change the protections you put in place. While ongoing computer training is always helpful, I am referring to significant jumps or changes in the way things are done.

Besides major upgrades, what other events might flag a re-examination of technology in the Lohrmann household? At least annually, something really new emerges in our family of six. High-tech Christmas toys get plugged into the home network, a daughter gets her first cell phone, or a family member starts using the Internet in very different ways. This prompts a jump back to Step 1, where we research and/or train those involved.

These technology steps may seem like a burden, but you can turn these activities into a fun training opportunity. Kids naturally want to know what you're doing online, especially if a new box of software or some cool new device has just arrived in the mail or from Best Buy or Staples. Seize the moment, and explain what's happening. I've found that those teachable moments often become instant impromptu family gatherings and opportunities to reenergize good Internet ethics.

Habit #5: Balance Online and Offline Life

In February 2008, The National Institute on Media and the Family website delivered this message: "From MySpace to Facebook to Xanga: The promise and peril of 'hanging out online.'"[21] The website urged parents to download their free guide to social networking, as well as their helpful guides to cell phones, online gaming, advertising, and more.

In her online resource, "Raising Digital Kids,"[22] Robin Raskin answers a myriad of parenting questions and identifies healthy activities for children of all ages to grow mentally, socially, and physically while balancing online and offline life. If only things were as straightforward for adults.

Technology has so transformed our home and work lives over the past decade that many are tempted to never disconnect. While the benefits of unplugging may not seem obvious, consider this research:

There were statistically significant negative relationships between time spent online and time spent with family, with friends, and with work colleagues. Meanwhile, the amount of time being alone significantly increased. . . . Home Internet use came directly out of interaction with family members while work Internet use was compensated by reduction in the amount of time spent face-to-face with co-workers. In addition, time spent using the Internet at both places concomitantly increased time alone, further substantiating that "Internet use, more than any other activity, isolates people from simultaneous active engagement with others."[23]

If you think this cultural trend will abate any time soon, think again. The already pervasive cell phone is gradually being upgraded to become a universal communication device that will become even more integrated into our lives and provide increasing (and seemingly essential) advice, commerce, entertainment, and virtual access.

While it is definitely true that e-mail, instant messaging, and social networking sites like Facebook can help facilitate communication among friends and work colleagues, I am constantly amazed by the miscommunication that can happen with technology as well. E-mail wars with coworkers sitting in the next cube, inappropriate IM comments to/from my daughter's high-school friends (that would never happen in person), and the exponential spread of hurtful gossip are just a few of the potential negative consequences.

Some technology companies, like IMlogic, recognize this danger and take steps to help.

The company provides all the corporate trappings you would expect from a high-tech firm: good salary, bonuses, option grants, three weeks' vacation time, full benefits and a strong corporate culture. It also hands out BlackBerrys, laptops and cell phones to employees. Shelley Kolesar, IMlogic human resources manager, said it makes workers more flexible and allows them to use their time more productively.

But Kolesar and IMlogic executives also stress the importance of disconnecting, with policies designed to help employees unplug and unwind, such as quarterly company events away from the office.[24]

My point: we need to constantly analyze when to use technology and when to turn it off. Since we all have blind spots, this is another area where conversations with trusted friends can help (habits 1 and 3). Each of us faces different temptations, and we all go through different seasons of life. There is no secret formula to get proper balance, but like the bushes in front of our house, without deliberate pruning, the Web will take over more territory.

Online Time Management

Just as taking pledges and making resolutions can help us succeed by articulating our goals, predetermined time limits can help us balance online and offline life. This approach is not just for kids. We allot times for meetings at work, services at church, golf tee-offs, attending sporting events, and other areas of life. Why not block off Internet surfing time?

So what are some more practical ways to help us unplug? Dr. Paula Eder, a time management expert, offers seven Internet tips; here are the first five:

1. Whenever possible, limit your time online to certain times of day.
2. Close your e-mail and turn off your instant messaging and RSS feeds.
3. Keep your goal in mind when you do Internet searches.
4. Keep a running list of interesting links you uncover.
5. Set time parameters for your task, so you don't get "Lost in Cyberspace."[25]

Jeremy Smith offers this additional advice at a Christian website for students: "Emotions and feelings can often affect your judgment. If pornography is a temptation for you, avoid surfing the Web when you are hungry, angry, lonely or tired. Go find someone to spend time with."[26]

Many families find that scheduling family game nights or couples date night is the only way to ensure quality time is available. And yet, the Internet can take up all of the "spare time" between activities. Although this is a tough habit to break, scheduling computer time can actually focus tasks and reduce temptations. I've found that holidays, vacations, business trips out of state, and other "downtimes" can bring added time and opportunity to wander. Remember the adage "An idle mind is the devil's workshop." Try to go the extra mile to plan fun, offline activities during vacations and holidays. When traveling on business, get out and see the city or visit a distant relative.

When I was growing up in Baltimore, my parents kept me "engaged" in a variety of sports and church activities—all the time. Don't misunderstand, I enjoyed going to every Vacation Bible School in West Baltimore every summer. It was just a little strange to be the son of a Lutheran pastor attending a Methodist, Baptist, Episcopal, Pentecostal, or even another Lutheran church's week-long events.

Once the parameters are set, there is a variety of timers and tools that can help—especially with kids. Some solutions, like the Bob TV/video game time manager from Hopscotch Technology,[27] will cut off power when the time runs out. To control access, kids must type in an authorized PIN. Time-Scout Monitor[28] has similar functionality but uses swipe cards instead of a PIN to control access.

Of course, careful thought and discussion need to be given to determining the maximum amount of time (and freedom) an adult or children should be allotted online. The website InternetSafety.com lists "10 Signs Your Child Is Breaking the Rules Online." Most of these signs also apply to adults. Here are four samples:

1. You or your child receives unusual amounts of unsolicited e-mail or pop-ups.
2. Your child tries to block the computer screen or quickly closes the window in which he is typing.
3. Your child spends an unusual amount of time online, especially in the evenings.
4. You discover inappropriate images or files on your computer.[29]

Merging Offline and Virtual Worlds

There are more and more areas of life that cross over into shades of gray—situations that start online but end as face-to-face meetings. This advice, given by an Internet dating service, actually applies to many other online matters.

> You can increase the chance of success by remembering one simple tip: Always be honest. . . . Do not lie. Be genuine. Be yourself. Online dating success relies on representing yourself for who you really are. The anonymity of the Internet allows people to embellish, leave things out, or even just create a whole new person. Inevitably, a first date will not work out when the people finally meet in person. It's much better to be up front with who you are and what you're looking for. This attracts the kind of people you want to meet. Even if you get fewer responses, the chances of a date working out and moving to a second date are greater.[30]

It's important to remember that contacts made online reflect our offline character. Acting politely is important, even when rejecting offers at work or establishing new connections. I've lost count of the number of times that I have had contact with people online and eventually met them at professional conferences, homeschool sporting events, church meetings, or other events. Make sure that your online words don't create future offline embarrassments.

Between church activities, community events, and busy work schedules, there never seems to be enough hours in a day. But if you are looking for wholesome offline family-oriented fun, Focus on the Family's "Focus on Your Child" website offers a long list of online ideas and offline family-centered activities that can help provide a proper balance in life.[31]

On the other hand, sometimes we just need to say no to new online commitments. Like most people, Thomas Wailgum, a busy editor for *Chief Information Officer* (*CIO*) magazine, was not looking for more things to do. He understood the many benefits of Facebook, and he was urged to set up his personal site by old friends and colleagues. And yet, in response, he decided against it; he wrote this in his professional blog:

At this stage in my career with the daily job demands and pressures, playing Scrabulous with my friends, listing all of the things I should have done today (but didn't) and avoiding messages (or "pokes") from old acquaintances I've not spoken to since high school just aren't going to be big productivity-enhancers for me. There's no doubt that Facebook can provide meaningful social connections; but it also can be a huge productivity killer. And that's what I don't need more of in my life.[32]

Wailgum may be on to something. Larry Chase predicts that some innovative travel agents will start to offer "Internet-free zones"[33]—with no cell phones, no Internet, no fax machines. Of course, you can always go camping with the family to get disconnected and back to nature. Or can you? The Sierra National Forest and the Yosemite National Park now have wireless Internet in their campground areas.[34] Other state and national parks and campgrounds will surely follow suit—but that just reconfirms our need to learn when to say yes and when to say no to technology.

One concluding thought on balancing online and offline life: an important answer in this area comes from our prayer life. I try to remember to say a short, simple prayer before I enter cyberspace—especially if I'll be researching and visiting many websites. Prayer shows deferential recognition that you're not just in a physical battle. There is a spiritual dimension to navigating cyberspace, and we need God's help. Which leads us to the sixth habit in faithfully navigating the brave new Web: practice humble authenticity.

Habit #6: Practice Humble Authenticity

Proverbs tells us, "When pride comes, then comes disgrace, but with humility comes wisdom."[35] Why humility? Quick, simplistic answers can't possibly compete with the well-thought-out methods that are constantly being deployed, enhanced, and updated by expert marketers in cyberspace. These Web gurus use metrics to gauge what works and what doesn't. Didn't click today? That temptation will be fine-tuned and slightly different tomorrow.

One clear pattern that repeats itself is this: pride often precedes problems regarding cyber ethics. The smarter the system administrator or computer guru, the more he or she will be tempted to beat the system—often by pretending to be someone else or acting unethically in anonymous ways. While there are many courses on being "cyber smart," there is no substitution for moral responsibility and godly character.

How does pride enter virtual life? While most people acknowledge that online behaviors can become unhealthy or addictive, many insist that the negative effects won't happen to them. Others have taken steps recommended by various experts to protect one's family—only to be frustrated by their lack of success at overcoming temptation. In either case, they surrender and give in to behaviors that violate their professed values, just as they might give in to chocolate cake while on a diet.

In his insightful book on living virtuously in the Information Age, Quentin J. Schultze describes how Václav Havel, the Czech Republic's incredible first president, who rose to power after years in a Communist prison, developed a humble perspective on life, which powerfully influenced how he governed. Havel cautioned the world in a 1990 speech: "We still don't know how to put morality ahead of politics, science, and economics. We are incapable of understanding that the only genuine core of all actions—if they are to be moral—is responsibility."[36]

Havel recognized his personal weaknesses and stated that everything worthwhile that he had accomplished was done to conceal guilt. "The real reason I am always creating something, organizing something, it would seem, is to defend my permanently questionable right to exist. . . . The lower I am, the more proper my place seems; and the higher I am, the stronger my suspicion that there has been some mistake."[37]

Schultze elaborates on how Havel's words can help our current perspectives on technology and cyberspace. Too often, we buy into the lie that science and technology will eventually solve all our moral problems, so we continue to engage in immoral activities while waiting for the next round of innovation to somehow help— or even to bring salvation.

If we take the time to reflect on our own situation, we might conclude that no amount of information technology is going to repair the destruction in our own lives. . . . We depend too much on technology to save us from a fall into fear. Only when we give up on our technological faith and accept the resulting fear can we truly act responsibly. . . . We should fear the informationism of our age because it lacks humility; it puts us in the business of authoring paeans to efficiency and control rather than first admitting our foolishness. Short-term technological setbacks, from power surges to hard drive crashes, should remind us that we are not fully in control.[38]

So how can we practice humble authenticity online? I'd like to suggest three practical ways:

1. Conduct honest self-examination
2. Stay away from the "virtual cliffs" in cyberspace
3. Surf your true identity

1. Conduct Honest Self-Examination

Just like Václav Havel, we need to honestly examine our current situation if we are going to be authentic. The goal here is not just some intellectual exercise or emotional catharsis, but to get help where needed. Do you have multiple identities online that you use to conceal your sinful, illegal, or unethical activities at home, school, or work? You'll benefit from counsel and accountability as you struggle with these quandaries.

The Abilene Christian University Counseling Center's website[39] provides a wide range of helpful resources and Web links to help. Whether you are looking for workshops, need counseling, or just want some more helpful links, I recommend visiting their site.

Other helpful sites include: Virtuous Reality[40] (for girls and young women), Men of Integrity[41] (for guys), Freedom Begins Here,[42] and Pure Desire Ministries.[43] "Pure Desire Ministry International (PDMI) is devoted to healing men and women who have become addicted to sexual behaviors harmful to their social, family and spiritual well being. By supporting local churches, PDMI is setting men and women free, so they can walk in the saving Grace of the Lord."[44]

In his excellent book *Future Grace*,[45] John Piper, pastor for preaching at Bethlehem Baptist Church in Minneapolis, addresses our need to battle sin by believing God's promises, which offer so much more pleasure and happiness to our lives than the sin we commit. Since we sin because of the pleasure that the action offers us, the key to destroying sin's power is to have "faith in future grace." His ministry website, which is named "Desiring God," contains this sample:

> What is future grace? It is all that God promises to be for us from this second on. Saving faith means being confident and satisfied in this ever-arriving future grace. This is why saving faith is also sanctifying faith. The power of sin's promise is broken by the power of a superior satisfaction; namely, faith in future grace.[46]

One practical strategy for battling lust that Piper uses in everyday life is called "ANTHEM." Here is what each letter stands for:

A Avoid the external allurements if possible.
N Say No within five seconds of the internal feeling of temptation.
T Turn the mind forcefully in another direction to another image and truth.
H Hold this image and truth firmly in your mind until it pushes the other out.
E Enjoy a superior satisfaction.
M Move into a useful activity from idleness or other vulnerable behaviors.[47]

2. Stay Away from the "Virtual Cliffs" in Cyberspace

Boundaries—everyone has them. Starting from our earliest days when parents and teachers protected us with rules like "Don't leave the playground" or "Stay away from the busy street," we've all had our limits—and desires to test those limits. Progressing through middle and high school, peer pressure brought more temptations to go in a different direction and test parental boundaries. Even as adults, we're still tempted to exceed speed limits or cut other corners in life to give us an advantage.

But when it comes to cyberspace, the number of gray boundaries grows exponentially. What does this look like? Entering chat rooms "to help" victims of an unfaithful spouse. Chatting on a dating website when married. Misrepresenting your background or credentials in an online résumé. Redefining "online research" to management at work. The list is endless.

Scripture tells us to flee from evil. Avoid known "hot spots," or recognized areas of temptation. Far from "dabbling in sin" or "just trying things out to see what happens," we should flee from these temptations. If we hang out near cyber cliffs, we will eventually fall over the edge.

Working out ethical details at work can become complex. There are certainly gray areas that require in-depth analysis. The Josephson Institute's Business Ethics Center[48] offers an abundance of practical guidance for those looking for the right actions to take at work. Here's a sample of some of the free material available at their website:

- The Hidden Costs of Unethical Behavior
- How to Improve Work Life with Ethical Behavior
- How to Harness Ethics to Increase Productivity
- Management Guidelines for Promoting Accountability

Many times we know the right thing to do, but we just choose to go the other direction. We misrepresent who we are, or our true intentions. The final aid to help you practice humble authenticity online is to surf your true identity.

3. Surf Your True Identity

What is truth? As we navigate the Web, we constantly face that same question that Pilate asked Christ. For travelers in cyberspace, the answer is more data, more choices, and a smorgasbord of options—so everyone can be happy and choose for themselves. However, for followers of Christ, who said, "Everyone on the side of truth listens to me,"[49] and who taught, "I am the way and the truth and the life,"[50] Internet answers can cause moral friction. Entering the

Web, Christians are often persuaded to challenge the relevance of Christ's teachings or other biblical truths.

This plays out in our home life with hundreds of TV channels and more websites than we could possibly visit. Our culture tells us that if you don't like what you're watching, just change the channel or surf somewhere else. However, advertisers deliberately place subtle temptations where they know they will be most effective at leading us to cross boundaries, resulting in integrity theft. So if you want to go somewhere or do something online that you know is wrong, society offers freedom to adults to create a new character that is not a Christian and let that avatar go "in your place." You can participate as an observer who is only "seeing what others are doing" or change your role or even adopt a totally new online identity. One compromise leads to another until we lose our virtual integrity. How can Christians counter this downward spiral?

One way is to overtly identify yourself as a Christian online. There are many scriptures to back this up. "Trust in the LORD with all your heart and lean not on your own understanding; in all your ways acknowledge him, and he will make your paths straight."[51] Jesus said, "Whoever acknowledges me before men, I will also acknowledge him before my Father in heaven. But whoever disowns me before men, I will disown him before my Father in heaven."[52]

Being an authentic Christian in cyberspace surely doesn't mean flaunting your beliefs, bragging about your faith, condemning others online, witnessing in sports chat rooms, or placing virtual bumper stickers all over the Internet. Nor does it mean announcing to everyone online that you're a Christian. But using offline life as a guide, a Christian label can affect your outlook and others' expectations.

The Sermon on the Mount challenges us to be salt and light in the world. It means being a humble, patient listener. Yes, people will watch your online actions. Colleagues will hold you accountable to a higher standard at work. If your identity is in Christ, you will surf differently. You will apply questions like "What would Jesus do?" in difficult circumstances. Your goals will be different.

Just as playing fun games offline sometimes includes play-acting as others, so in cyberspace, we sometimes will act as imaginary characters. Yes, there are times when anonymous posts or pseudonyms make safety sense, and your accountability partner(s) can help you figure out appropriate boundaries. The key to all of this is openness, transparency of actions, preventing deceptive situations, and not using anonymity as a means to evil.

In conclusion, practicing humble authenticity online will strengthen your character and counter many of the tempting strategies you will face in cyberspace. You will gain a healthy understanding and confidence that dangers are often packaged in new ways, and you'll avoid cyber cliffs. At the same time, you won't fear the virtual worlds you do enter. Best of all, you will receive blessings from above. "God opposes the proud but gives grace to the humble."[53]

Habit #7: Become a Cyber Ambassador for Good

Once an authentic Christian identity is clear, what should characterize our demeanor as we interact in cyberspace? How can we make a positive difference on the Internet? If we don't place our ultimate trust in technology to save us, what outward expressions will help us maintain our virtual integrity and at the same time help others online? The last habit is to become a cyber ambassador for good.

In a series of outstanding vision papers, Redeemer Presbyterian Church in New York City provides an excellent model for us to follow. The first paper lays out their key beliefs.

> The gospel is the good news of gracious acceptance. . . . The gospel is the good news of changed lives. . . . The gospel is the good news of the new world coming. . . . This pattern creates an "alternate kingdom" or "city" (Matt. 5:14–16) in which there is a complete reversal of the values of the world with regard to power, recognition, status, and wealth. When we understand that we are saved by sheer grace through Christ, we stop seeking salvation in these things.[54]

Redeemer's last vision paper focuses on Christians and culture. Far from running away in fear or hiding from others in the "big, bad city," this is a vision of engagement. While Redeemer addresses its attention on New York, I believe the same truths can apply to our focus on the virtual worlds in which we live.

1. Christians should live long-term in the city. . . . People who live in the large urban cultural centers . . . tend to have greater impact on how things are done in a culture. If a far greater percentage of the people living in cities long-term were Christians, Christ's values would have a greater influence on the culture.
2. Christians should be a dynamic counter-culture in the city.
3. Christians should be a community radically committed to the good of the city as a whole. . . . In the end, Christians will not be attractive within our culture through power plays and coercion, but through sacrificial service to people regardless of their beliefs. We do not live here simply to increase the prosperity of our own tribe and group, but for the good of all the peoples of the city.
4. Christians should be a people who integrate their faith with their work.[55]

Redeemer has taken this fourth point and truly put its vision into action, launching the Center for Faith and Work (CFW) in 2003, and making a positive difference throughout New York City in a wide variety of professions. While some may decide to move to New York City and join Redeemer, how can the rest of us apply this vision to redeem our corner of cyberspace? Dr. Mike Wittmer, associate professor of theology at Grand Rapids Theological Seminary, says everything we do matters to God.

Christians must accept a double responsibility for God's world. Because we are humans, we gladly unite with other people to develop culture, joining the upward climb from the pristine garden of Genesis 2 to the organized city of Revelation 21. Besides this cultural mandate, our commitment to redemption also inspires us to stay alert for those points where our culture is misused for evil purposes.[56]

Building on Redeemer's vision of redeeming the city, and Dr. Wittmer's book *Heaven Is a Place on Earth,* I'd like to offer four brief ways to become a cyber ambassador for good.

1. Be prepared—know your orders
2. Speak the truth online
3. Offer servant leadership by transforming your community and Webspace
4. Opt in to e-fun—adopt a sense of online humor

1. Be Prepared—Know Your Orders

Christians need to be biblically trained prior to becoming cyber ambassadors. I believe this is a huge challenge for families, churches, and Christian schools. Yes, there are many books on cyber-savvy surfing and avoiding online predators, viruses, and other traps. What is needed is a biblically based moral curriculum that addresses both children and adults in cyberspace.

Just as President John F. Kennedy's promise to put a man on the moon motivated NASA to study and prepare in new ways for space travel, the exciting new promises offered by Bill Gates, Eric Schmidt, Steve Ballmer, and other technology leaders should prompt each of us to prepare in new ways for interactions in cyberspace.

By definition, an ambassador represents the government of a nation. Ambassadors speak with the authority and the protection of the sending country; and yet, their words are not their own. While there is flexibility in how the message is delivered, the message comes from the president or prime minister. In the same way, our Christian message needs to reflect the truth from God's Word. It takes experience, wisdom, and training to effectively deliver the appropriate, nonpreachy message at the right moment.

So we'll never be faithful and effective cyber ambassadors of Christ if we aren't grounded in Bible study and good teaching. If you are not getting good Bible teaching that is relevant in your life, I urge you to go online and use the Internet to access some of the inspirational teaching available from Tim Keller, John Piper, or other helpful preachers.[57]

2. Speak the Truth Online

Most online situations at home and at work do not present the opportunity or necessity of an outward expression of my Christian faith. At work, I deal with 1,001 different topics online, from personnel issues to installing new software to late projects. Yes, my Christian faith informs these topics, but the majority of readers of my CSO blog probably don't even know that I'm a Christian. I still have many opportunities to proactively speak the truth on the Web.

Unless you work at a Christian company or church, your virtual interactions are probably similar to mine—without much mention of God. And yet each of us has numerous opportunities to speak up for justice and truth and the "right things" on home and work networks. Our informed conscience should be our guide for when to listen and when to challenge the status quo. This means speaking out against inappropriate Internet/intranet activities at the office, steering conversations in chat rooms in a positive direction, or just offering a helpful hand to the elderly at our church who are having PC problems.

I believe that we can be actively engaged in redeeming cyberspace by supporting positive activities that encourage online and offline virtue. If we are proactively seeking opportunities to be agents of good "IRL" or "OT" ("in real life" or "out there"), we will be obediently fulfilling Christ's commands to his followers. This is hard work, but it is our calling. To paraphrase Martin Luther, "God milks his cows by those farmers assigned to that task."[58]

3. Offer Servant Leadership by Transforming Your Community and Webspace

When the Ford Motor Company wanted to improve teen driver safety, they turned to a YouTube-style video to preach driver safety. New tips are posted at their cool website, which has sections for parents, students, and educators.[59] They've even taken their video-clip messages to sites like YouTube, MySpace, and Facebook.

There are an infinite number of ways that tech-savvy kids, teens, and adults can utilize Web technology to make a difference. From building websites, organizing fundraising efforts for the needy, or helping churches with their community programs, we have just begun to apply technology in powerful ways that can transform our communities, schools, workplaces, and homes. Every time a new innovation appears on the scene, there are opportunities to apply the technology for good.

A Google search for "Christian Web ideas" brought over half a million results in February 2008. So if you're stumped for ideas, make this a family research project. Getting involved online can also help build valuable experience for young men and women who want to enter a technology profession.

There are a number of effective organizations that are designed to help families navigate the many challenges that they face in twenty-first-century life, including the Internet. One of these Christian organizations is BRAVEheart. Its website describes the organization this way:

> BRAVEheart Teen Initiative is a non-profit Christian organization that promotes an abstinent lifestyle to reduce the risks of unwanted pregnancies, sexually transmitted diseases, and emotional trauma. BRAVEheart uses the participation of teens and young adults in the form of teams to encourage today's youth and single adults to make healthy decisions in regard to their sexuality.[60]

BRAVEheart holds events like father-daughter "purity balls," which include ballroom dance music and instruction, special entertainment and gifts, a tea reception, and a program including a father-daughter covenant. Since these special events are expensive, BRAVEheart also holds fundraisers to help defray costs. Real-world events sponsored by organizations like BRAVEheart can help immensely in establishing the right offline support regarding cyber pledges and Internet purity.

4. Opt In to e-Fun—Adopt a Sense of Online Humor

Everyone wants to have a good time. Surfing the Internet should stay positive, with more dos than don'ts. Opt in to e-fun—go after positive things OT. Our cyber experience will definitely be enhanced if we can laugh at ourselves, relax, and not be so serious. I love this quote: "We've all heard that a million monkeys banging on a million typewriters will eventually reproduce the entire works of Shakespeare. Now, thanks to the Internet, we know this is not true."[61]

An occasional visit to websites like Cleanjoke.com or cybersalt. org/cleanlaugh is just what many may need to lighten the mood around the house and have some fun with the kids. As mentioned earlier in balancing online and offline life, there are plenty of other websites that promote family and workplace fun.

In conclusion, Quentin Schultze nicely encapsulates the attitudes and substance behind the seven habits for surfing your values that I've just outlined: "To be virtuous people in a high-tech world is to be neither moralists nor pragmatists but sojourners who humbly seek goodness in an eternal adventure that began before we were born and will continue after we die."[62]

9 ➡ What If?

2012, a Cyberspace Odyssey

Technology can be seen as a bit impersonal and create distance between the guest and the [hotel brand], but in reality it can help in reestablishing and personalizing the experience. We are using technology to break through that clutter and noise and reconnect with the customer. Technology gives us a new kind of intimacy and allows [the guest] to be brand loyal because it helps recognize the consumer wherever I go.

Jonathan Tisch, Chairman and CEO of Loews Hotels[1]

It was the week before Christmas 2012. I had finally ordered the last of our presents online a few days earlier. The hustle and bustle of parties and church events that seem to overwhelm every December had finally ended. The kids had just gone to bed on a cold, snowy night, so I sat down and enjoyed a cup of hot tea in my favorite chair.

As I thought back over the past month, I recalled my recent trip to Chicago. After enjoying a few moments of peace, I felt compelled to sit down in front of the computer. I wrote this letter:

Dear Hotel Tomorrow Management and Staff,

I want to thank you for the outstanding service that I recently received when I visited Chicago. I was especially impressed by the remarkable improvements you've made over the past year to personalize my experience and make me feel right at home by honoring my values.

I checked into the Hotel Tomorrow on Weds., December 5, 2012. What a difference from last year! I knew you were one of the first hotels in the country to implement your new "We Value Your Values" campaign. Before my trip, I was able to input my values inventory with just a few clicks from Google's new "e-Values" website. I had no idea how much you could do with that information. As I entered the room, one of my favorite songs was playing in the background. Nice touch, and just the first of many tech-savvy surprises. After I unpacked my bags, I enjoyed a hot cup of my favorite tea while I finished reading an article from my favorite magazine that was sitting on the table.

I was able to quickly and easily use the "My Entertainment" feature on the TV. I appreciate the fact that you provided the family-friendly channels that I value without any awkward discussion at the front desk. I was also glad to see that you subscribe to the Fox Network's new personalized programming with "Integrity Advertisements." What an improvement that makes in TV! I'll be subscribing to that service at home, and my son and I should be able to watch a baseball game together without turning off the commercials.

I usually hate traveling. I'd rather be home with my family. I didn't know how you did it, but the digital pictures of my kids in the room were awesome. Actually, I found out later that my wife sent the photos to my room over the Internet. My eight-year-old daughter's pretty smile reminded me of my real priorities. Enabling me to watch that short video clip from my son, Paul, on Thursday evening (about his first basket ever in a "real" game) was just the lift I needed after a long, hard day.

You even hit a homerun with the 20-percent-off "digital coupon" waiting for me from my favorite Chicago restaurant. The auto-reservation system was awesome. I didn't realize that you partnered with local restaurants. I had a great dinner and saw an old friend at the same time.

I don't normally write these types of letters. In fact, the only other letter I've ever written to a hotel was to complain. I just had to let you know that your customer satisfaction efforts through personalization are working wonders. I've traveled to five-star hotels around the world, but this was my best experience ever! I'm actually looking forward to my next trip to Chicago in the spring. I'll bring my family, so they can see the Hotel Tomorrow for themselves.

Keep up the excellent work!
Daniel J. Lohrmann
Michigan Chief Information Security Officer

Just Fiction?

Seem impossible? Most of the technology exists right now to make this values-based encounter a reality. Remember Loews CEO Jonathan Tisch's words: "We are using technology to break through that clutter and noise and reconnect with the customer."

This is a "what-if" vision. Since I can't predict the future, the exact dates, the hotel, and even the city are unclear. Still, this type of experience can happen in the near future. It may be more like 2015 before we get there, but that depends on how big a priority this becomes in the next few years. My hope is that this kind of experience is widely available for travelers within five years.

How can this become real? Our number one task as Christians and others who want to surf their values is to organize an effective campaign that gains the necessary industry priority. Primarily, we need Microsoft and/or Google (or perhaps other computer and Internet giants not yet born) to see the need and implement their version of this picture. We also need media companies like News Corporation (parent of Fox) and other media companies; hospitality providers such as Loews Hotels; and the many media, hospitality, travel, technology, and entertainment businesses to catch this vision as well.

There are ways to move to Plan B or Plan C if Google and Microsoft and other existing companies don't want to participate. Still, getting the Internet powerhouses to lead a values-based online experience is the best way to make a scene like this available by the end of 2012 (or sooner).

Why would these companies want to do this? The market is already heading in this direction. That is, a massive movement toward personalized, one-to-one communication on the Net is emerging. These companies want to know your values and dreams so that they can provide better, more customized service and keep you coming back. They also want to target various niche markets in better ways and "get inside your head" so they can match product advertisements to individual and family needs.

Consider this quote from a leading consultant in hotel innovation: "Americans are living in a post-scarcity environment. Meaning, whatever someone wants can be easily purchased so having a particular product is no longer special. This is rapidly changing the consumer mindset and they are now seeking more intangibles, which is emerging as the desire to have unique experiences. Technology is a vital tool in helping to facilitate experiences. . . . You have to trust your customers. Don't tell them what they want. Ask them what they want."[2]

At a simplistic level, consumers need to ask for new "family values" or "faith-based" options from their ISP, high-speed cable company, software providers, hotels, and other businesses. Google and Microsoft are primary because they are the two main forces in Internet technology right now. They control the two biggest entry points to reaching online content. In the future, the Internet will connect much, much more than today, and additional companies will need to respect customers' online values as well.

Jesus said, "You are the light of the world. A city set on a hill cannot be hid. Nor do men light a lamp and put it under a bushel, but on a stand, and it gives light to all in the house. Let your light so shine before men, that they may see your good deeds and give glory to your Father, who is in heaven."[3] I believe this call to be light has never been more vital than today. As cyberspace becomes more and more integrated into our lives, there are unique opportunities to be light in the world and not hide under a bushel.

You may wonder how churches and individuals can be a city on a hill that cannot be hidden in cyberspace. Christians and others who want to surf their values need to work together in a variety of ways that support a values-based Internet—and not just rely on politicians or technical experts to do the right thing. In the appendix, I'll discuss some national strategies to help, but government legislation is actually Plan C, which I hope is not necessary. Economics 101 courses teach us about the reality of supply and demand, and we need the clear demand. I know Christians (and millions of others) already want these kinds of options.

This values-based scenario is by no means guaranteed. One essential question is, Whose values will we be surfing? We need a groundswell of bottom-up support to create this market for wholesome content. There are powerful forces who want all of us to keep watching tempting commercials that undermine traditional family values and chip away at our virtue. Many people in the entertainment and media food chain are making money from the current model, and they have plans to spin more bad stuff our way. They benefit from hiding in shades of gray that allow them to capitalize on sinful desires that are bad for individuals, families, and society.

Cyber Hedges

Living virtuously requires us to build practical protections around marriages and families. Jerry B. Jenkins wrote a book in 2005 entitled, *Hedges: Loving Your Marriage Enough to Protect It.* Jerry lists many practical ways that he protects his marriage, including care in meeting, dining, or traveling with women other than his wife. Whether married or single, each of us needs his or her own list of "hedges." In fact, you may not realize it, but most Christians already have many natural hedges around their lives to protect them from various forms of evil in the "real world." These God-given gifts include family members, friends, positive activities at home and church, and even the physical distance away from tempting activities. Businesspeople know that traveling presents a set of temptations that people who are at home with their families do not face. Like the prodigal son, as we pull away from these protections, we become more susceptible to temptation and various evil influences.

Most of these protections are absent in cyberspace, and we need to build healthy new "e-hedges" into our online experiences. I'm not just talking about filters to block unwanted content. We need renewed minds and new habits. And we also need new online mechanisms that support our faith, families, and marriages.

Independent faith-based groups and others need to provide input and direction to companies like Microsoft and Google. We fill out consumer surveys on likes and dislikes every day. From flower shops to airlines, companies know our preferences. Information about the things we care about is also provided to political parties, churches, and even job-finding websites like Monster.com. This type of information would be in your values profile to enable customization to work. The public will be able to decide whom to use as their service provider and how much information they feel comfortable disclosing. It will also allow new companies to emerge with innovative solutions.

While evaluating online content is the part of the vision that is perhaps the hardest to coordinate and implement, it should be noted that a variety of mechanisms can personalize content today, using a variety of factors. We currently give ratings for games and movies. Numerous groups, including the federal government, faith-based groups, and the movie industry, already have roles in discerning appropriate content labels. For example, both *World Magazine* and "Plugged in Online" (from Focus on the Family) currently rate movies for their worldview and family-friendliness. Extending this practice to Web content is a natural progression.

New Technology

Until recently, the challenge of labeling all Internet content was impractical. However, we now have a new technology protocol, called "XML," that makes tagging content an essential part of the process used by content management systems to produce

Web pages. These tags can be very specific, and can allow every image, video clip, even every word or phrase to be categorized with a label. Not only will websites be categorized to a greater degree in the future, but everything you see within a portal or Web channel will be tailored (or targeted) to the specific tastes of the user based upon some profile. Content can already be resized to be displayed on TVs, phones, BlackBerry phones, and a variety of different input devices,[4] but personalization will go much further in the future.

Another important technical advancement has occurred in search technology. For example, Google has a technology called "Sitemap protocol," which allows Google to dig much deeper into databases and other content and make that information available online in an easy-to-find manner. This approach has enabled Michigan and other states to greatly improve their citizens' search capabilities. In fact, today's incredible search technology is perhaps the major advance that makes surfing your values more than a dream. Microsoft, Yahoo, and Ask.com have also made great advances in their search technology.

My point is that we still have time to make this a win-win situation as we enter into a new period in which high-definition digital TV and the Internet's content-delivery system are being reinvented. The approach I'm advocating will not be forced on anyone, but it is an option available to all as part of what the courts call "personal responsibility."

There are good people who want to offer genuine options to keep sections of cyberspace out of the moral gutter. The next battle will not be about the 10 percent of content on the good and bad extremes, but the other 80 percent of content in the middle. As more people express their desire for clean entertainment and other Web content, dollars will flow in that direction.

What Are Google and Microsoft Thinking?

Eric Schmidt, Google's chief executive, was interviewed in May 2007 in London about his view of Google (and cyberspace in general) five years from now. "The goal is to enable Google users to be able to ask the question such as: 'What shall I do tomorrow?' and 'What job shall I take?' . . . We cannot even answer the most basic questions because we don't know enough about you. That is the most important aspect of Google's expansion."[5]

So Google wants to help plan my life? They even have dreams for me? That's interesting. I never knew they even knew the Lohrmanns existed, much less cared. By the way, Bill Gates, Steve Ballmer, and other cyber gurus have made similar statements.

But before we scoff at or dismiss these comments, remember that these are very smart billionaires on a mission. This may initially sound as scary to you as it did to me. Are you ready to terminate that high-speed connection? Should we boycott these "evil empires"? My answer may surprise you.

I say no. Rather than fight these developments, I recommend working together and making this a win-win situation. I believe Christians can and should work with Eric Schmidt and Steve Ballmer to make significant progress in implementing new opportunities with family values.

Naturally, I don't believe that an Internet venture should be picking my next job, planning my week, or even selecting my favorite restaurant in Chicago. However, they can certainly provide very useful information, bring in valued opinions from experts I respect, and draw convenient maps with pictures. I could even value seeing some ads for restaurants near an out-of-town meeting that offer coupons to first-time customers. Their programming gurus who build mind-boggling search engines can also start to help me stay away from tempting content and links that are bad for our moral health and deliver just the answers needed based upon my values.

I think that these technology leaders want individual users to have more control and freedom as well. Here's a quote from Steve Ballmer from 2000: "The Internet today, I would argue, is 100 percent backwards from what it will be 10 years from now. Today, the Internet is largely in the control of website producers, not the users."[6] Their connected vision can actually do many good things and help us eliminate unwanted temptations—if we get this right.

Back to the Future: Imagining a New Values-Connected World

Perhaps you're wondering how Google, Microsoft, a hotel—not to mention your TV or computer—can possibly know your values. To make this clearer, let's take another quick "what-if" journey back into the near future.

Blog entry for Dan in "Christian Living Today Online"—October 23, 2012:

> I went to a conference on the future of cyberspace down at the University of Michigan in Ann Arbor last week. Some guy from Google gave the keynote address, which I must admit was really fascinating. The best part was their new e-values approach, which allows massive personalization on searches and more. In some ways, Google (or its competitors) will become "the camera lens" through which we will see all the content on the Internet. The cool part was the collaboration that will be enabled by joining this service. This approach will affect everything from watching TV, to visiting a hotel, to seeing ads. Basically, my entire set of interactions online will change. Microsoft will probably launch their alternative approach soon.
>
> At first, I thought this was a little frightening. If I go along, they'll know everywhere my family goes and everything we do online. But I remembered that I "google" just about all my questions anyway. They already have that information. They also have our e-mail accounts, and we're moving more and more of our information and services over to them all the time. Even many of our work tools, like spreadsheets and databases, are stored by Google or Microsoft, although many businesses have a different privacy arrangement with both Google and Microsoft.
>
> Google, the company, has become "google" the verb. I rarely go straight to websites anymore to search through their pages; rather, I use a search engine to get straight to specific answers. This approach could really help. They promise improved search capability, heading toward true weighted answers, based upon my values inventory. They also announced partnerships with hundreds of other online companies (and thousands more to come) which will enable my e-values profile to personalize my services and the content that I see at most websites. From buying things online to preferences when

I travel in real life, I will be able to centrally manage most virtual relationships.

I raised my hand and asked if there would be a default (or easy-to-select) "Christian profile." To my surprise, the answer was yes—although they call it "faith-based values." There are multiple ways to easily personalize how pure you want to be, on a scale from 1 to 10 for static content or "G" to "R" for interactive content—like movies. A 10 would effectively mean you're open to "XXX" content. They said you will even be able to personalize your experience for the different (major) religions such as Christian, Muslim, Hindu, etc.

Anyway, I decided to take the bait and become a part of their final beta test. Using the information they gave me at the conference, I easily linked my current Google e-mail account to their "e-values inventory." WOW! Yes, this gets a bit personal, but I also started to see huge value in what they are doing. I was so impressed!

This was e-Harmony on steroids, but not just about finding a mate (or a date). Many areas are optional, but I decided to take the long version of their "scientific" questionnaire. They had some standard templates available to choose, with boxes to select like "strong religious convictions" or "morally conservative," which they claim you can use to finish in under five minutes. Still, since I wanted to see what was behind each category, it took me almost thirty minutes to answer a hundred questions.

I was really fascinated by how they deal with reputation-based selection of websites and content. It reminded me of how RCI (my timeshare condo company) grades resorts in categories, such as gold crown, silver crown, etc., as well as which services they provide. By allowing communities to grade suppliers of information and provide feedback, they can offer more helpful content to various focus groups. This is similar to, but better than, the way Wikipedia works. For example, if information on a website was deemed to be unreliable or misleading "gossip," it would receive a low reputation or be deleted. This approach discourages misleading content in the same way we do in the real world. If someone has a bad reputation, we take their words less seriously.

You'll really like the red, yellow, and green light option that can be activated to change colors when instant messaging or chat room conversations are seemingly violating professed values. If video clips or other content is "suggestive," but not porn, a yellow light pops up. That feature also uses the context, content source, IP address, and other technical data to determine whether fraud is likely to occur when buying something or if a transaction cannot be trusted.

By the way, I really like the little "e-Me" picture—an avatar (or online character) representing me. While waiting for content to download, my e-Me starts scratching his head or looking at his watch. When I went to a new site, he started walking to the new place. You can even turn on your "online conscience," which asks your avatar questions when you potentially go through "yellow lights" that tempt professed values and beliefs. There must be a bit of artificial intelligence in there, since my online conscience learns my actions and likes and dislikes—but he's not perfect. My "red-light" actions definitely violate professed values, and that content is not even offered as a temptation—unless someone sets their profile up differently than I did. By the way, my daughters will love buying clothes and more online for their new e-Me.

Besides external appearance, the inventory of topics for my e-Me include moral values, religious beliefs, character, education level, age, my trusted sources of online information, and so much more. It was a little like taking a career guidance test, but more about values and beliefs. There were even questions for "healthy lifestyles," which included dieting and exercise questions, which a friend I know will appreciate, as a recovering alcoholic.

Other helpful features include their transparency and accountability options. In a nutshell, they offer a variety of ways to discuss your choices and profile with your spouse, friends, and/or work colleagues—which I recommend. (You're allowed up to ten accountability partners.) Once the profile is saved, any changes will result in an e-mail being sent to your accountability partner(s), alerting them of the changes.

This is where the "enabling integrity" piece applies. The software allows surfers to "say what you'll do and do what you say." The nice thing about this feature is that your accountability partners only need to see changes in your profile once it is "approved" and not see long reports on every site you visit or every link you clicked on. Partner companies like Symantec and Websense can even ensure that all surfing happens through your profile, no matter how you go online.

They even made interactions fun and practical by allowing you to see and communicate with a circle of friends and family avatars on a regular basis without losing your privacy to stranger avatars. It's clear that their goal is to emulate "real life" by letting you reveal just what you want to others. That is, you can be anonymous to some and even have pseudonyms, while allowing others to be very close to you and even be accountable to them. The approach reminds me of natural interactions and allows trust to build slowly but cautions against potential dangers online. For example, when my family goes to Disney World, we don't know most of the people, but we can still interact at a certain level. The conversation changes with friends at church or colleagues at work, etc.

Yes, the proof is in the pudding, and these values profiles dramatically changed everything about my online experience. Once I activated the values settings, the Google desktop was completely different, and my favorite places and things to do were right on my desktop with a simple click. As I searched or went anywhere on the Internet, I felt as if they really knew me, because they did. The interface wasn't perfect, but surfing will never be the same. Oh yeah, and it was fast too.

Back to Today: A Model to Surf Your Values

You may be thinking, "I want it." And yet you don't see how we can possibly get to this type of experience in just a few years. I believe that the main thing is to lay out a clear vision that values-minded people can get behind. We also need to brainstorm on new Bible-based ideas for implementing family values as we put together this new roadmap. In pragmatic business terms, we need to lay out the high-level requirements for a model to better equip and encourage Christians to surf their values. I welcome others to join me in perfecting this near-term model.

It may seem unrealistic to hope that computer and Internet companies can be coaxed or coordinated into more support of value-based surfing. This is a big dream or vision, and it does face many challenges. But technological developments and online possibilities are already headed in a direction that makes virtual integrity and customized surfing feasible. So where do we start? First, a few assumptions:

Assumption #1: "They" (online service and product providers) want to know what "we" (their customers and users) value, and "we" want to surf our values. They want to market (sell) "us" stuff—and that is how cyberspace will be (primarily) funded and grown. Depending on the results of the "net neutrality"[7] debate, we may pay for more services.

Assumption #2: "They" will provide the required security, privacy, and service level. I'll take this up in more detail in the next chapter. Mistakes will be made along the way in these categories, and trust will be broken by some. Still, the market will drive business to partners that provide true "family-friendly, morally safe solutions."

Assumption #3: New partnerships will be needed. New protections and laws may be needed. I'll say more on this in the appendix.

Assumption #4: "They" will need to include many other companies and service providers in addition to Microsoft and Google. There are myriad technical and business-model possibilities in this space. Hotels, airlines, TV and computer manufacturers, and others will join technology companies in engaging in this process. However, at the current time, Microsoft or Google are best positioned to lead this charge and drive the required change. Therefore, they need to help us "surf our values" in the same way that the Kellogg Company changed its marketing strategies, as described later in this chapter.

Assumption #5: "Christian values" (for that religious orientation within the "we") need to be clearly defined. There are a variety of good answers to this problem; however, we'll never get to just one answer (nor should we). There are many different religious perspectives and beliefs, and even denominations who have differences in their values. Still, there are many common areas of agreement on temptation.

Various groups can help define the required details around initial default profiles.

How Can This Happen?

In the simplest terms, Google or Microsoft will really "know" (have detailed profile information on) each member of the Lohrmann family when we opt in to surf our values. Just as our pastor, real estate agent, or personal tax adviser knows us, future software companies will know our values. We will fill out a detailed profile, in a similar way that some current dating sites match people via profiles today or as we fill out a personality or career counseling profile.

This new system can also know our preferences about everything from clothes to foods. (Values and preferences will likely be two different categories.) More importantly for Christians, we will be able to indicate very specific categories of content that we do not want to see. Unlike the current situation, content will not simply be "blocked" in the same way we block certain websites or links. Rather, content will be delivered to us in just the way we want it, based on search results with detailed parameters on what we are seeking. The optional transparency features built right into the process will serve to reinforce our goals in the same way that members of Weight Watchers gain support from others in the program who hold them to account.

Online content will be available via multiple "input devices." That is, the same profile will be portable whether you are using a PC, BlackBerry, home TV or entertainment system, game console at home, office PC, hotel entertainment system, car entertainment system, school PC, university PC, or anywhere else the Internet can be accessed.

How will search engines and other central sites know so much? Remember that most of the questions that are answered online today come when you "Google it." People get to the content via massive databases that the companies create by "crawling" (or literally examining every possibility) through cyberspace and keeping track of everything they see. The secret lies in the search engine's ability to quickly get you the most relevant answers to the questions that you ask. One current drawback is the thousands (sometimes millions) of answers that are given. Most computer users want more specific answers to the questions they ask, with fewer alternative answers.

These new searches will reduce the amount of data we're seeing. Future searches will likely provide the option of very specific answers or the opportunity to see many alternatives. Again I ask, whose values will be used when those specific answers are given? If users of Google, Live, Ask, or Yahoo won't provide background on their values, someone else's values will be used as a default. There's really no middle ground. For example, if you type in "beach vacations," there are a wide variety of perspectives and values that may go into the options presented. The results could show everything from family resorts to pictures of nude beaches.

The simple truth is that the more search companies know about you, the better they can provide what you are looking for online. Currently, you can set a few different "filtering levels" during searches—but this approach is not even close to satisfactory. Don't forget that content can be in the form of text, pictures, video, or voice (via a podcast), and can be "resized" into larger or smaller chunks depending on preference or the device you're using. For example, a phone browser will display a long letter in smaller chunks than will a large computer monitor—which may show the entire letter. Security considerations are covered in the next chapter.

This leads to an important benefit for those living "open and transparent" lifestyles. Google and Microsoft will be able to help you surf your values much easier than someone who is hiding who they are, where they are really trying to go, and what they are really trying to do. Many of the people who ostensibly want "privacy protections" are protecting sinful lifestyles and habits that they want to hide from others—sometimes including family members. I'm not suggesting that all privacy protections are bad, since there are many times when privacy is essential and valued. But the key is to provide the option to enable more integrity and let those who want to reduce temptations stay accountable to trusted friends and family. This new experience will also allow more informed, thorough answers to questions in cyberspace.

While there can be benefits to surfing anonymously, there are clearly more temptations to act "out of character." If I want to enable true online integrity, I need to verify who I am before I can "say what I do and do what I say." These same new options will help protect children.

While it is not right to lie or deceive in cyberspace, there are times that a pseudonym (or anonymous public presence) is appropriate. For example, we don't want to give personal details to online predators. One good guide is to ask ourselves the simple question, How would I behave in the "real world" if faced with the same situation? In this model, our surfing profile is known to those closest to us (including the parents of minors), but only a part (or none) of our values profile would be known to strangers we meet online. The "just enough" rule will apply to social interactions online. How much the other person knows about you can be controlled by the user.

Another important benefit that jumps out at Christians is a "new beginning" to think through their online values with those they love before setting up their detailed online profiles. The benefits of working through a well-thought-out plan should be self-evident. This process alone will help overcome appeals to engage in unwanted distractions and opportunities to head toward sites lying, cheating, stealing, and promoting various forms of lust.

Plan B

What if Microsoft, Google, or another key player will not support this vision? While this is possible, I think it is unlikely—due to their professed desires to get to know us better and "do no evil." A more likely scenario is verbal agreement with slower implementation of values-supported surfing.

And yet they could reject a faith-based or values-based experience. Fortunately, there are other search engines, such as "Ask" or "AOL" that many people use to surf the Net. Table 10 shows the Web search market share in early 2008. In addition, companies like Symantec and Websense are leading fighters in the filtering and security battles in cyberspace. Others such as Facebook, MySpace, AT&T, Sprint, Verizon, or another company could emerge with new ways to help "surf your values."

Company Name	Market Share
Google	77.11
Yahoo	12.23
MSN—Global	3.43
Microsoft Live	2.59
AOL—Global	2.13
Ask—Global	1.42
Other	0.24

Table 10. Web Search
Market Share—January 2008[8]

Might Ask or AOL become the "champion of family values" in cyberspace? Could this issue become the distinguishing difference that moves their (or another competitor's) market share up? It is definitely possible. In reality, I suspect that plans A and B will happen simultaneously. However, Google or Microsoft could reject these concepts and fall behind in what I believe is a core issue globally for individuals, families, and businesses. I must reiterate that Christians and others who want to surf their values need to rise up and make their views known for these companies to engage.

Plan C

Someone is bound to ask, "What if no technology companies participate? Isn't it possible that none of these companies will take the steps that will enable us to surf our values anytime soon?" Again, I think there is only a very slight possibility of this happening. If this situation develops, legislation and government intervention is Plan C. I'd rather not see the need for this approach, but mandated protections for families by federal, state, and local governments could come. Although some laws regarding cyberspace decency have been ruled unconstitutional in the past, an opt-in set of protections can be upheld in the same way that protections have become law for secondary smoke from cigarettes. Australia and other countries are mandating filtering protections for children, and this is a logical next step.[9]

There is plenty of precedence for state and federal legislation regarding cyber activities. There are numerous federal, state, and local laws and ordinances protecting us from identity theft and discouraging the spread of pornography, deceptive behaviors, and fraud. Americans don't like porn stores in their neighborhoods, nor do they like online predators. I have no doubt that Plan C would work, if required. Technology companies would have a very hard time standing up "against family values" in the name of "free speech" if this is an optional program. But again, government intervention is a last and least desirable alternative. I'll discuss more on a national strategy and legislation in the appendix.

Kellogg Example Points the Way

Actually, there many examples of large-scale adjustments made by major corporations in response to the deeper interests and values of their customers. Consider the problem of obesity in America. As Americans "supersize" their diets and eat sugar-coated cereals, it has been predicted that 75 percent of us will be overweight by 2015.[10]

Of course, this trend has scary implications for our nation's future health. In response, a variety of parents and health advocacy groups have pulled together and started to brainstorm possible new solutions. Groups like the Center for Science in the Public Interest even threatened lawsuits against companies that were marketing products to kids under twelve. In June 2007, Kellogg Company issued a press release[11] which provided details of major new initiatives. These initiatives provide new product standards, marketing standards, and even changes to website designs and automatic screen timeouts for children.

What's the new normal at Kellogg? Healthy lifestyles and balanced diets are the new "cool" messages being pushed. What's out? Images of food in computer games, file downloads, and wallpaper that don't meet the new criteria. Kellogg's commitments "began immediately" and will be completed by the end of 2008.

That's quite a change. I remember growing up watching cartoons with commercials for "Kellogg's Sugar Frosted Flakes." Those became "Kellogg's Frosted Flakes" at some point, as sugar was deemed a bad marketing word. Now, the colorful messages are changing again as the marketing world admits they were culpable, albeit with their actions and not with their words.

In the early part of this decade, McDonald's started to get the same message from the public. They started to change the way they presented almost everything on the menu. Their stock price and sales even started to rise after they marketed "healthier" alternatives. At the same time, fast-food alternatives like Subway began to grow as they marketed low-fat subs and weight-losing-customer examples.

How did this change occur? Again, in the case of Kellogg, parents got together and rose up to demand meaningful change to the status quo. If corporate and other changes can be prompted to better our children's breakfast habits, why are they not also possible to enable and reinforce our virtual integrity, to help us surf our values?

Of course, this vision brings up many questions. While I can never anticipate or address all the likely questions, I'm dedicating a chapter to filling in some of the holes. Please join me in digging a bit deeper into this "brave new Web."

10 ➡ Brave New Web

A Flood of Questions

Live in Your World, Play in Ours

Sony Playstation Trademark[1]

The brave new Web is already here. Millions of people are drawn further and further into new virtual experiences every day. Just as Americans wander through the Mall of America's seemingly never-ending number of stores, we explore new parts of cyberspace—but without leaving home. Whether having fun or chatting with others around the world, we seem to be never satisfied with the last experience.

So we must step back and ask questions. We need to analyze our current experience. As Christians, we need to examine our hearts, our motives, and online desires. Once we agree on the roadmap, we can start to implement a new path. When Google's director of mobile platforms, Andy Rubin, was asked whether the phone companies will fight Google's new phone offerings, he responded simply, "Consumers are demanding change."[2] Nice response, Mr. Rubin. In fact, exactly the same is true in terms of consumer hopes and desires to be able to surf their values.

In the preceding chapter I tried to sketch out a vision of a Web designed so that those of us who want to can opt in to virtual integrity.

Of course, I realize that there are many questions about this potential new direction. Is this really the right destination? Why should we spend our valuable time and scarce resources to pursue these goals? What are the pros and cons for security and privacy? In this chapter I want to turn to these and other important questions, many of which may have already occurred to you as you read chapter 9.

Preventing Censorship

As new approaches are considered, we must remember that the United States Supreme Court struck down provisions of the Communications Decency Act (CDA). This 1996 law was deemed to restrict free speech on the Internet and online services. David R. Bender, executive director of the Special Libraries Association (SLA) said this about the ruling: "This decision will have a major impact on our society's development and use of electronic communications for decades to come. . . . SLA believes that personal responsibility and parental control are the answers to the problems addressed by the CDA, rather than onerous government intervention at the expense of the First Amendment."[3]

Moving forward, a clear goal should be to stop the ongoing "race to the bottom" regarding cyber morals that is affecting everyone. Still, I'm not suggesting the elimination of immoral content, but rather the delivery of the content that people desire—based upon their values. Free speech is protected, but there is no constitutional mandate that we must listen to everything being sent, any more than I must allow those who plan to harm my children into my house. In fact, privacy rights and consumer laws ensure an ability to be protected from intrusive spam and other unwanted material. Rather, the offer of a new set of content delivery alternatives for those who want to surf their values is now within view.

In a recent book, Dinesh D'Souza describes the majority view in the Muslim world regarding moral decadence in America. While Americans see more traditional societies as too harsh and supporting of censorship, Muslims consider it better to uphold public moral standards, even while falling short, than to relinquish standards that can't always be met. "Muslims may be hypocritical and support censorship, but these facts provide no basis for a defense of Western cultural depravity. . . . Muslim leaders charge that Western culture has no moral norms that it is willing to defend or uphold."[4]

Protection of free speech must be maintained as we move forward in cyberspace, but we must also protect the other rights of Americans, such as freedom of religion. We also need to be sensitive to the global aspects of cyberspace that go beyond U.S. territories. New solutions need to incorporate the values of the diverse voices in society, while enabling families to pass down religious values with adequate controls.

Are the Existing Christian Options Enough?

As a matter of fact, there are several excellent Christian Web portals, and new services and portals are being developed all the time. Christianet[5] was the most-visited Christian marketplace site in 2007. I also like The High Calling[6] and Faith in the Workplace[7] from *Christianity Today* for work issues and related topics. Plugged In Online[8] from Focus on the Family is a great site for movie and game reviews. For Christian social networking, there are many sites like Godtube, Xianz,[9] and Lights Together.[10] However, there are many problems with just focusing on these sites to address online integrity and morality.

First, Christians don't go to them as exclusively as many might like or think. We use Google, Yahoo, Live, or Ask to get to the content we're looking for online. Many Christians use MySpace, Facebook, YouTube, and other popular sites for everything from social networking to getting their local news. We also visit blogs, weather.com, USAToday.com, WebMD.com, and a huge list of other cyber destinations.

Second, using exclusively Christian sites won't truly impact our experience at hotels and other mainstream industries. Bottom line, America goes to Wal-Mart and not ChristianMart, both offline and online.

In addition, I could list dozens of technical and other reasons why these sites alone can't implement the comprehensive vision for virtual integrity that I've tried to articulate in this book. That being said, many of these portals are great resources to visit, and they help us engage other Christians. They provide a vision of what a Christian experience can be in areas like social networks. In one sense, they provide part of the "To Be" vision right now, so I encourage support of these online places.

What about Privacy and Security?

There is little doubt that the 2012 scenarios presented in my previous chapter will raise privacy and security concerns. Many squirm at giving this kind and amount of information to companies like Microsoft and Google. Entire books have been written on privacy concerns, and the European Union and many other countries are putting new privacy notification rules in place. The fear of identity theft and a long list of other crimes has created entire industries to enable the good and fight the bad. In fact, that is probably why a chief information security officer is writing this book.

Ever since starting my professional career at the National Security Agency in 1985, I've spent my life working on network and information security issues. I've researched numerous aspects of our privacy problems and written extensively on security topics. We have a long way to go. We probably won't arrive at a totally secure Internet in my lifetime. Still, the Internet is moving forward, and we need new approaches to solve urgent problems.

Personal information is just that, personal. Unfortunately, it is also all over the place. Governments have our data, but so do Wal-Mart and Blockbuster Video. Banks, credit bureaus, hotels, churches, schools, and a myriad of other institutions know just about everything there is to know about us. Ever Google yourself? The Internet knows quite a bit about you as well. Like it or not, this trend will only grow as we move deeper into the twenty-first century.

As a result of the security breaches and headline stories regarding identity theft, credit card companies and governments are now taking cybersecurity very seriously. I fully expect that the millions of dollars that companies are currently spending to resolve security breaches will bring improvements in the cybersecurity situation over the next few years. Still, home users need to take steps to protect themselves now, and I outlined those steps and current resources to help in chapter 8.

Despite my belief that these issues can and will be addressed, I realize that some will never be comfortable answering the kinds of questions that will allow them to truly surf their values. But I want to point out that sites like e-Harmony are successful because millions of people feel differently. Obviously, their members are willing to share personal information with a company in order to find a life partner. Others get help with their taxes from those they trust, get career advice or counseling online, or even share information with wider groups on social networking sites. Since millions of people already use credit cards for almost everything they buy online and offline, their banks know quite a bit about their values.

I challenge critics with this question: Will you stop others who want to opt in (without being coerced) to have a different experience based upon their beliefs? Please don't get me wrong, I do of course believe we must protect sensitive information and ensure privacy controls—after all, I have spent my entire professional life building and refining network security in systems and organizations and enabling privacy. We just need to figure out how to incorporate our values into the equation as well, for the good of individuals, families, and society. Remember that the level of sharing values can be tailored to individuals.

Basically, most people want to know: What are you doing with my information? Who can see it and who can't? Who has access to my data? Clear privacy notifications must be sent from companies to customers. Legal protections on misuse must be enforced. In addition, security breach laws, requiring public notice of a compromise, are now commonplace and should be retained or strengthened.

Different Values-Sharing Models

Should our information be centralized, decentralized, or a mix of both? One counterargument to this vision goes something like this: Yes, Blockbuster Video, my cell phone company, my church, my grocery store, and others have information on me. But Blockbuster knows my taste in movies, my church has different data, and the grocery store has yet another set. What you're proposing would group eating, film, religious, and all kinds of other habits and preferences in one place.

I believe that providing Google, Microsoft, or another trusted technology partner the centralized information they need regarding our personal values makes sense in return for the many benefits. This assumes the proper service-level agreement and legally binding privacy protections are in place. However, I want to be clear that there are several ways that this vision can also be realized in a decentralized manner. (See table 11 for a summary of the possible centralized, decentralized, and mixed models.)

First, I want to advocate for the centralized approach. Personally, I'd rather have a centrally stored and trusted databank than a myriad of small retailers trying to secure my private information. Why should we trust these Internet giants? Companies like Microsoft, Google, and AOL, and even computer security experts at Symantec and McAfee, understand the global Internet security situation far better than most. They "get it" when it comes to the necessary ongoing vigilance regarding Internet threats to misusing my data and, more importantly, the solutions available. Many businesses have a hard time protecting information, because it is not their core competency. They don't take this security task as seriously as they should, nor do they apply fixes fast enough to keep up with the "bad guys." Microsoft and Google also have the most comprehensive view into our virtual world from different platforms—including cell phones.

While competition and consumer options are essential, more centralization of sensitive data is coming anyway, as a result of our current identity theft crisis. Over the next few years, we will see new identity management systems emerge both at home and at work. As more and more transactions in society become digital, new, easy-to-use authentication and validation systems will gain widespread adoption. These advances will be driven by governments, banks, and other financial institutions that are hearing customer demands to reduce fraud and identity theft, by new technology that provides far more power in smaller devices.

Profile Model/Description	Positives	Negatives
One centralized (main) profile—Microsoft, Google, or others manage relationships and pass information to others	Easiest to use, implement; greatest incentive; security breadth covers all interfaces and Internet; fastest adoption	Perceived privacy concerns; may harm further competition
Mixed model (several) profiles—ISPs, search engines, large tech providers have profiles	More competition; more companies interested	Can't reach all Internet access (ISP doesn't see work); more complex
Decentralized model (many) profiles—most like today	Perception of more privacy (information in many places)	Security more difficult; hard to sync data; less convenient
Centralized model—(independent) third-party owner of profile	Trust of independent provider; provides benefits of central approach without giants	Slowest; least incentive for Internet giants

Table 11. Profile Models

Decentralized profiles on each of us already exist, and they are being expanded. For example, you may have heard about how people in Japan already use their cell phones like credit cards to make purchases, from sodas in machines to lunch at restaurants. As discussed earlier, this trend will massively expand the functionality of the cell phone to include more Internet-connected areas of life, from GPS to TV.[11] The name will change from "cell phone" to something like "advanced technology access manager" or "ATAM." (My wife and daughter want to name it "Eve" for "Everything Virtual Enabled.") My point is to think about how much information our cell-phone providers already have on each of us—which will only grow in the future.

Several entrepreneurs, like Adam Jackson,[12] describe how social networking and cell phones are just starting to come together. In November 2007, Motorola bought into Australian social networking site Tilefile Limited;[13] Nokia has made similar moves and prefers the label of "Internet company."

This newly developing reality creates decentralized opportunities for virtual integrity. Perhaps our internet service providers or next-generation cell-phone-service providers can provide us an opt in values-enabled option. Indeed, ISPs are already getting into this market behind the scenes.

Internet service providers have begun using or testing technologies that track their subscribers' online activities and serve ads based on those behaviors. . . . "I don't think people realize how fast these companies are moving," said AOL's [Dave] Morgan. "They're moving fast. Now there's going to be a big question about how many of the big ISPs play."[14]

Let me be clear: I am against targeted ads that are implemented without consumer consent or with only an opt-out mechanism. I advocate for privacy and for letting consumers know what is happening with their information or surfing habits. In December 2007, the FTC issued guidelines for self-regulation on behavioral advertising. "Every Web site where data is collected for behavioral advertising should provide a clear, concise, consumer-friendly, and prominent statement noting that (1) data about consumers' activities online is being collected . . . and (2) consumers can choose whether or not to have their information collected for such purpose."[15]

Rather than secretly gathering information on consumers in the background, the vision presented in chapter 9 takes the concept of behavior-based ads and goes much further, to the benefit of family values. Rather than companies guessing what consumers want, we get to opt in and specify our values and not rely on others to try and impose their values on us. This also limits unwanted temptations, which current behavior-based solutions don't. Simply stated, current approaches go too far for some by building unwanted profiles that many consumers consider to violate their privacy. And yet they don't go far enough for values-based customers that want to truly surf their values.

Besides a very centralized approach or a more distributed approach with different profiles held by ISPs, cell phone providers, Wal-Mart, or others, there is another possibility. Trusted, independent, third-party keepers of our profiles could be established. These entities would serve as our agents as we interact with various Internet portals and various virtual services. In the same way we can give the power of attorney to others, these groups may eventually provide the right amount of virtual information to others, depending upon the situation and need. They could act as brokers, in much the same way that eBay is a broker online today in online auctions or credit agencies provide information on us. This concept would take the longest to develop, since it offers the least return on investment for companies like Google and Microsoft.

Incentives for Internet Companies?

One of the biggest and most apparent roadblocks to such a vision is that it requires considerable input and cooperation from powerful corporations such as Microsoft and Google. Furthermore, these companies are bitter rivals. What if they come up with incompatible (technical and platform) solutions to surfing our values? Is it really reasonable to expect competing companies to work together coherently enough to enable the comprehensive virtual integrity we've imagined in chapter 9?

I think it highly likely that Google, Microsoft, and others will have different solutions. The tricky part is how that works with our TV, hotels, and other companies. We may see partnerships in the future that drive loyalty, in the same way that frequent flyer miles drive loyalty to airlines today.

There's no doubt that a "standards-based" approach that provides a common format is easiest for consumers. Still, we've faced these dilemmas for years with different formats for everything from video cameras to computer game consoles. Only time will tell if we end up with multiple solutions or one set of "protocols" with different interfaces.

On the other hand, competition can also be good for users. It can drive innovation and pressure companies to offer niche solutions. The fact is that the technology industry has been dealing with this interoperability issue for years, and we will continue to build new connectivity that works as long as there is a customer need. Many people are saying that we will soon be talking to our ovens and refrigerators on our way home, to turn on our dinner or learn that we need to pick up more milk. If this is true, we can certainly pass what we value to a hotel. In short, different solutions can hurt the cause by making things more complicated but can help by offering competition and alternatives.

Compatibility and interoperability issues aside, it is abundantly clear that all Internet companies desire to have "stickiness," or a close ongoing relationship with customers that will keep them coming back. Building loyalty through customer service is now the name of the game in all businesses and industries. Loyalty bonus programs, targeted discounts to repeat customers, and automatically generated orders are the kinds of techniques that online (and offline) retailers such as Drugstore.com and Petco.com now use frequently.[16] Even my local gas station has a loyalty program. The bottom line on loyalty is that companies want to know what you value (and buy), to get you coming back for more.

The urge to know and satisfy the customer or user is even more acute for online operations. "Use psychographics more than demographics," says Rob Frankel, a well-known author of several books on Internet websites and branding. "Psychographics has much more to do with people's likes, attitudes, inclinations," Frankel explains. "In traditional offline mass media . . . demographics will work OK. [But] the web is completely flipped."[17]

In other words, the targeted (one-to-one) audience is what makes the Web experience radically different from traditional advertising, where you throw out (or broadcast) your nets to everyone in hopes that you catch enough fish. It is important to note that MySpace and Facebook already use information that is placed in profiles to target ads. Perhaps one of them, or a startup company, will play the central role. I'd advise them to partner with an established search company with ties to the marketing world.

What about the "Bad Guys"?

I've said we're in an arms race online, and otherwise devoted considerable attention to Internet dangers from those who act with unsavory or even malicious motives. So what about companies that might misuse my information to actually send materials that violate my values? Won't others ignore my preferences and keep sending tempting spam and worse?

As I insisted earlier, integrity theft and identity theft are "partners in crime." While we will never get to 100 percent control of those who to try to steal in various ways, there are millions of people and billions of dollars being spent to resolve cyber crime. Although this is a hard battle, many in society are already eager to win this fight. We need to partner with them and be trained to recognize false appeals, tricks, and illegal marketing scams.

The search companies are best positioned to know what is what and to keep us clear of the "bad stuff" online. They can use reputation-based analysis and other techniques to go around the bad guys and not allow the improper messages into messaging systems. Simply stated, the "bad actors" will keep trying to divert you to the bad parts of cyberspace, but the powerful maps of the Internet will be owned by the big search companies. This fact makes it imperative to partner with companies that have the "cyber roadmap" if you want to traverse the Internet with virtual integrity.

It is important to realize that many temptations are coming from reputable first world companies that are not currently incorporating values into their Web marketing. These companies want to get to know you better, but just as in any productive relationship, there needs to be mutual respect for it to work.

The main thing is to agree on our online goals and the right destination before we dwell on the illegal activities of the minority. A huge benefit to using a reputable search engine as a front end to the Internet is that they have cataloged what's out there for us. Therefore, they can help us avoid sites that are known bad actors.

I also expect that new security and privacy solutions and approaches will eventually reduce unwanted spam in cyberspace, probably within the next five years. Adding values to your experience will actually help reduce unwanted spam and other content that violates stated expectations. The security companies play a part in this battle, and they will likely offer ways to enhance our experience as we surf between portals. Our governments, financial institutions, and others have vested interests in solving this problem.

So cyber crime will never disappear, but that is no reason to fear the future. We each need to take security seriously today and take steps to protect ourselves. Surfing your values will help protect you online in the same ways that we stay in safe parts of town in the real world.

A Christian Response

Paul said, "Finally, brothers, whatever is true, whatever is noble, whatever is right, whatever is pure, whatever is lovely, whatever is admirable—if anything is excellent or praiseworthy—think about such things. Whatever you have learned or received or heard from me, or seen in me—put it into practice. And the God of peace will be with you."[18]

There are a variety of ways to engage others through cyberspace—especially with the new Web 2.0, where interaction is king. Believe me, the editors of these online resources notice what people are saying and seeking. Constructive input affects their future discussion topics, articles, and final product. If we follow Paul's words in Philippians 4:8–9, we will reap the benefits of that wonderful promise: "And the God of peace will be with you." I think that our greatest solution to e-temptation is to have God's presence within us as we surf.

I believe that as Christians we need to be engaged in redeeming cyberspace and not retreating from these important topics. That can start right now with your interactions online. Start a blog on a topic that you're interested in and provide a Christian perspective, comment on an online newspaper article, provide your views on a political campaign, or send an online postcard to one of the numerous travel websites and mention the excellent church that you attended on Sunday while vacationing.

Christians can surf the "brave new Web" without fearing the future. Sure, you will encounter opposition, but if the early Christians faced lions, we can certainly engage today's cyber culture with whatever is excellent or praiseworthy.

→ Appendix: Toward a New National Strategy on Cyber Ethics

Democracy without values turns into an open or thinly disguised totalitarianism.

John Paul II[1]

On May 10, 2006, President George W. Bush issued Executive Order 13402, which established the Presiden t's Task Force on Identity Theft, "a strategic plan aiming to make the federal government's efforts more effective and efficient in the areas of identity theft awareness, prevention, detection, and prosecution."[2] In April 2007, the task force reported back to the president. Its executive summary begins this way:

> From Main Street to Wall Street, from the back porch to the front office, from the kitchen table to the conference room, Americans are talking about identity theft. The reason: millions of Americans each year suffer the financial and emotional trauma it causes. This crime takes many forms, but it invariably leaves victims with the task of repairing the damage to their lives. It is a problem with no single cause and no single solution.[3]

Led by attorney general Alberto Gonzales, this presidential task force not only delivered an excellent plan but brought together an impressive list of experts from government, law enforcement, the private sector, higher education, national associations, nonprofit think tanks, and many others in a national discourse. They heard from consumers and businesses across America that were affected by this national ID-theft epidemic. The challenges ahead are immense, but the best and brightest are on the job—with a high national priority.

America needs a similar national discussion on *integrity* theft. Call it a National Strategy on Cyber Ethics, with a charge to produce a strategic plan for promoting family values online. Sobering trends and new technology have emerged that require this discussion to take place immediately. Just as this nation debates important ethical issues in medicine separately from health care for the uninsured, we must address cyber ethics as a related, but not subordinate, issue to our important cybersecurity battles.

In this appendix, then, I want to provide ways that individuals and groups across society can help the country onward and upward in its cyber ethics.

How Can Individuals and Families Help?

What practical steps can you take?

1. Make a pledge of integrity. Implement the seven habits to faithfully navigate the brave new Web in your own life. (See chapters 7 and 8 for details.)
2. Sign the online petition "Respect My Values" at www.virtualintegrity.org. This petition encourages new options for family values in cyberspace. Our goal: a million digital signatures on a letter to be presented to our 44th president, Congress, Google, Microsoft, Yahoo, Ask, and other major technology companies.
3. Write your federal and state political leaders (the president, Congress, state legislators, and others). Tell them to support action on Internet decency and cyber ethics in schools. Write to Microsoft, Google, and Yahoo, and tell them you want new

online experiences that allow you to surf your values with
integrity.
4. Get involved in your church or community group to help others
with cyber ethics.
5. Pray for family values online, locally, nationally, and internation-
ally.

How Can Technology Providers Help?

Rather than force legislative responses, the tech companies have the
best opportunity to change cyber ethics in culture through creating
new online experiences. What practical steps can tech companies
take?

1. Read chapters 9 and 10. Pour research dollars into family-values-
based experiences for customers that give customers what they
want in content and targeted advertising.
2. Engage in international standards discussions that allow experiences to be portable and yet secure as customers interact with
various businesses. (One example is going from Google to my
online bank to a "real" hotel.)
3. Engage Christians, those of other religions, and religious organizations in ethical discussions regarding virtual worlds and
new computer-human interactions.
4. Work with governments and other partners in establishing a
new national strategy plan for cyber ethics—in addition to cybersecurity protections.
5. Continue to train the world in technology, with an emphasis on
social responsibility.

How Can Businesses Help?

Large businesses around the world are just starting to understand the
new possibilities and new dangers that cyberspace will bring over the
next decade and beyond. If you think off-shoring jobs is a big deal,

wait for virtual worlds and the transformational processes that the Internet will bring for home, work, and our global reach.

Here's what C. G. Lynch, publisher emeritus of *CIO* magazine, said about a Forrester report on virtual worlds: "In five years, enterprise versions of online virtual worlds like Second Life will be just as important to business as the Web is today, and the trend will make it useful for companies to begin experimenting with 3-D online environments for in-house collaboration projects."[4]

Meanwhile, most businesses are struggling with the current ethical issues in technology. No business wants to stifle innovation or end up in a lawsuit over a hostile work environment. This leads to five suggestions for today:

1. Start a new internal discussion between management, human resources, and select employees regarding cyber ethics and your acceptable use policy. Use "participatory design" (PD) principles to get input from frontline staff as well as all parts of the business to discuss home/work issues and Internet life in the next decade. Use these guidelines:
   - Respect the users of technology, regardless of their status in the workplace, technical know-how, or access to the organization's purse strings. View every participant in a PD project as an expert in what they do, as a stakeholder whose voice needs to be heard.
   - Recognize that workers are a prime source of innovation, that design ideas arise in collaboration with participants from diverse backgrounds, and that technology is but one option in addressing emergent problems.
   - View a "system" as more than a collection of software encased in hardware boxes. In PD, we see systems as networks of people, practices, and technology embedded in particular organizational contexts.
   - Understand the organization and the relevant work on its own terms, in its own settings. This is why PD practitioners prefer to spend time with users in their workplaces rather than "test" them in laboratories.

- Address problems that exist and arise in the workplace, articulated by or in collaboration with the affected parties, rather than attributed from the outside.
- Find concrete ways to improve the working lives of coparticipants by, for example, reducing the tedium associated with work tasks; codesigning new opportunities for exercising creativity; increasing worker control over work content, measurement, and reporting; and helping workers communicate and organize across hierarchical lines within the organization and with peers elsewhere.[5]

2. Start thinking about how to brand content and not just your websites. "Associated Press CEO Tom Curley made an important and far-reaching keynote speech to the Online News Association Conference on November 12, 2004. In it he said, 'content will be more important than its container in this next phase [of the Web]. Killer apps, such as search, RSS and video-capture software such as TiVo, to name just a few, have begun to unlock content from any vessel we try to put it in.'"[6]

3. Ensure that employee values, including personal faith, are not violated in the overall mission, visions, and values discussions for your company, nonprofit business, or government organization.

4. Look into new forms of accountability for Web surfing of employees as part of security and privacy programs. Consider ways to enable, not disable, productivity and personal growth. Just as companies like IBM reward employees for good eating habits, reward good surfing behaviors. (See "Companies Rewarding Workers' Healthy Habits."[7])

5. Encourage technology vendors to offer new values-based approaches to product delivery.

How Can Churches Help?

Most churches are just starting to address the Internet behaviors of their congregations. While many churches now have a website, most offer limited or no training on cyber ethics from a Christian perspective. This needs to change. Here are five recommendations:

1. Offer training for Christians online. Tailor classes to be age-appropriate. Offer weekend retreats or evening seminars to discuss cyber ethics from a Christian worldview. Find a good curriculum and make this fun, interactive, and consistent.

2. Encourage accountability, as discussed earlier. Ensure that church staff have appropriately addressed virtual integrity. Encourage men's and women's groups to address this topic. Work with national organizations to utilize appropriate resources.

3. Reach out to the community regarding cyber ethics. Work with schools and other community organizations. Bring in experts to offer seminars on consensus topics. (See national examples to help.[8])

4. Pastors—preach and teach on biblical aspects of home and work that relate to your Christian faith—including cyberspace. Look at Redeemer Presbyterian in New York or other churches for models for redeeming your local community. Pray for cyber ethics in the country and your community.

5. Encourage those interested to join national efforts to transform the Internet and encourage family values and virtual integrity. Join national efforts as a church, where appropriate. Give to national efforts as appropriate. Encourage those performing outreach online and missionaries who use the Internet to adopt the seven habits listed in chapters 7 and 8.

How Can Nonprofits, Christian Companies, and Think Tanks Help?

1. Make cyber ethics a priority, first for your own staff and second for your research and lobbying efforts.

2. Provide appropriate funding and staff resources to address this effort. Working with institutes, foundations, family organizations, coalitions and governments, encourage more research and focus on Internet activities that encourage faith-based,

and/or family-based, Judeo-Christian values. (See Kaiser Family Foundation.[9])

3. Encourage your technology vendors and ISPs to offer new services that encourage family values. Groups like the World Council of Churches Commission on Faith and Order,[10] The Faith and Family Television Task Force,[11] and the Wabash Center for Teaching and Learning in Theology and Religion[12] can have significant worldwide influence in many spheres.

4. Two different groups—the faith-based community and the Internet Keep Safe Coalition[13] need to come together. Our tendency is to treat cyber ethics as less important, but we need a joint, national wake-up call. What's the goal? Just as a new coalition formed to urge action on border control, this group needs to lobby industry and government for changes in online family values. (See "New Coalition of Christians Seeks Changes at Borders."[14])

5. Develop curriculum and other resources to help Christians surf their values in a variety of ways and circumstances—with coming virtual worlds and new technology.

How Can K–12 Schools Help?

1. Establish a cyber ethics curriculum in your school. Bring character development into the classroom in relevant ways. (See Character Counts,[15] the CyberEthics Project,[16] and StaySafe Online.[17]) Discuss cheating and other rules related to technology with students.

2. Bring in outside experts to speak on cyber ethics and the Internet in general at rallies and assemblies.

3. Engage parents and the community in a dialogue on cyber ethics. Using the Parent-Teacher Association (PTA) or other groups, establish best practices and understandings for home and school. (See "Cell Porn Scandal Hits Pa. High School."[18])

4. Ensure school staff and students are protected with the appropriate software/hardware. (See Tools for Teaching Cyber Ethics.[19])

5. Examine new technologies and processes to benefit from values-based experiences.

How Can Universities and Research Institutions Help?

1. The universities and the academic research community need to provide staff, students, and others in their community with the appropriate ethical guidance and tools to do their jobs based on *The Ten Commandments of Computer Ethics* developed at the Computer Ethics Institute:

Thou shalt not use a computer to harm other people.
Thou shalt not interfere with other people's computer work.
Thou shalt not snoop around in other people's computer files.
Thou shalt not use a computer to steal.
Thou shalt not use a computer to bear false witness.
Thou shalt not copy or use proprietary software for which you have not paid.
Thou shalt not use other people's computer resources without authorization or proper compensation.
Thou shalt not appropriate other people's intellectual output.
Thou shalt think about the social consequences of the program you are writing or the system you are designing.
Thou shalt always use a computer in ways that ensure consideration and respect for your fellow humans.[20]

2. Working with groups like EDUCAUSE,[21] aggressively research new techniques and processes in cyber ethics.
3. Hold conferences, seminars, and other opportunities for students, professors, and citizens to be trained online and in person on technological issues related to cyber ethics.
4. Make cyber ethics a funding and resource priority among the many grants and research opportunities available to students and programs.
5. Open new programs in information assurance, and ensure that all professionals take ethics courses related to their field of study.

How Can Media and Advertisers Help?

1. Offer more excellent programs based upon family values. (See the Axiom TV example.[22])
2. Offer targeted ads based upon family values. Encourage opt-in technologies to do the same.
3. Police companies in your own industry (via federations and associations) that don't follow the rules. If nothing is done, legislation is coming.
4. Provide easier-to-use and better training for the public.
5. Work more closely with groups like the Dove Foundation and others to achieve these goals. Note these statistics:

   - 94 percent believe that offensive material in TV, movies, and the Internet is on the rise.
   - 93 percent want to see more wholesome family entertainment made.
   - If more were made, 84 percent said they would make an effort to watch and support it.
   - 77 percent stated that 75 percent of today's entertainment does not meet their expectations or reinforce the values important to them.
   - 70 percent said that the amount of sex, violence, and profanity in films bothers them.
   - 76 percent think that movie ratings have gotten too lenient, and they don't trust them. (This varies significantly from a survey by the MPAA that shows that 76 percent of the people they polled find the ratings somewhat to very helpful.)[23]

How Can Government Organizations Help?

1. Establish a national strategy on cyber ethics. Bring together all of the right stakeholders to drive answers and change. Follow the model from the ID Theft Task Force.
2. Establish a (largely symbolic) "ambassador to cyberspace" with the Federal Trade Commission (FTC). Follow Australian and

other national models to make protections the default in software, and make turning off protections an option, without violating free speech protections. (See "Conroy Announces Mandatory Internet Filters to Protect Children."[24])

3. Provide additional research funding for cyber ethics. Include significant funding for state and local governments, faith-based organizations, and national nonprofit groups to train citizens, along with national Internet efforts.

4. Political leaders need to talk more about cyber ethics and other family values topics in layman's language (as opposed to accounting lingo regarding regulations) in schools and other public venues. Use the bully-pulpit to encourage honesty and integrity and character. Walk the talk. Institute acceptable use policies for the Internet along with filtering at all levels of government, to show citizens that governments are setting the example and acting above reproach.

5. Aggressively deal with cyber fraud and its causes at all levels of government. Pass legislation to help protect the Internet and cyber citizens if corporations fail to act.

In conclusion, despite efforts to date, the online situation is currently deteriorating. Despite many positive efforts to address cyber ethics, this topic is not yet a top national priority. It needs to be. Using New York City as a model, we need to stop the individual moral indiscretions and crimes if we ever hope to solve the many larger crime issues in cyberspace. Most importantly, families are being impacted now.

The billions of dollars being invested in our nation's critical Internet and technology infrastructure will be for naught if a new concerted effort is not made to correct our course regarding cyber ethics as a nation. There are significant roles that each segment of American society needs to play in order to address our current cyber ethics situation. The implications of cyber ethics go beyond the use of the Internet. The very fabric of our future society depends on this battle. Actions online invariably lead to actions in real life. The time to act is now.

➡ Notes

Introduction

1. Mother Teresa prayer, Institute of Metro Ministries, www.bimm.org/Resources_BitsNPieces.php.

Chapter 1 Integrity Theft

1. Matthew 6:13 (ESV).

2. Calum MacLeod, "China vaults past USA in Internet users," *USA Today*, April 20, 2008, www.usatoday.com/tech/world/2008-04-20-Internetusers_N.htm.

3. "21st Century Skills—A Digital-Age Economy," Learning Point Associates, www.ncrel.org/engauge/skills/ageecon.htm.

4. Jack Powers, "Tempting the Click," *Journal of the International Informatics Institute*, June 15, 1996, www.in3.org/articles/tempt.htm.

5. O'Reilly Radar Online, August 23, 2007, http://radar.oreilly.com/archives/2007/08/peak_google.html.

6. Jeordan Legon, "E-mail greeting card hides porn," CNN, November 1, 2002, http://archives.cnn.com/2002/TECH/ptech/10/28/security.net/index.html.

7. Pete Thamel and Duff Wilson, "Poor Grades Aside, Athletes Get into College on a $399 Diploma," *New York Times*, November 27, 2005.

8. Paul Boutin, "How to Steal Wi-Fi and How to Keep the Neighbors from Stealing Yours," *Slate*, November 18, 2004, www.slate.com/id/2109941.

9. Searches conducted in January 2008.

10. Linked In, www.linkedin.com.

11. Larry Chase, "Top 10 Trends for Marketers," www.wdfm.com/trends-internet-marketing.php.

12. Scott Buresh, "Current and Future Search Trends: What the Top Internet Search Engines Are Doing," Internet IT Business Net, October 31, 2007, http://internet.it businessnet.com/articles/viewarticle.jsp?id=219977.

Chapter 2 Why Filtering Is Not Enough

1. HeartQuotes: Quotes of the Heart, www.heartquotes.net/Einstein.html.

2. See www.staysafeonline.org, www.ikeepsafe.org, www.onguardonline.gov, www.microsoft.com/protect/family/activities/social.mspx, or www.michigan.gov/cybersecurity for information on this topic.

3. FilterReview, www.filterreview.com.

4. "Technical Ways to Get around Censorship," www.rsf.org/print-blogs.php3?id_article=15013.

5. See "Tor Overview," http://tor.eff.org/overview.html.en.

6. See Vauhini Vara, "Ten Things Your IT Department Won't Tell You," July 30, 2007, http://online.wsj.com/article/SB118539543272477927.html. Also, an open letter to *WSJ Online*, http://blogs.csoonline.com/an_open_letter_to_wsj_online.

7. Jamie Stockwell, "WiFi Turns Internet into Hideout for Criminals," *Washington Post*, February 11, 2007, www.washingtonpost.com/wp-dyn/content/article/2007/02/ 10/AR2007021001457.html.

8. Kim Hart, "New Media Strategies' 'Online Analysts' Scour the Web for Mentions of Opinion-Sensitive Clients," *Washington Post*, January 29, 2007, www.washington post.com/wp-dyn/content/article/2007/01/28/AR2007012801032.html.

9. Message at http://controlyourtv.org.

10. See www.v-chip.org.

11. The TVBoss.org, www.thetvboss.org.

12. Plugged In Online, www.pluggedinonline.com.

13. Job 31:1 (NIV).

14. Craig Kuhl, "Campaigns, Tools Seek 'Sanity, Not Censorship,'" *Multi-Channel News*, www.multichannel.com/article/CA6386013.html.

15. *Paradise Hotel 2*, MyNetworkTV and Fox Reality Channel, 2008.

16. See Common Sense Media for detailed descriptions and helpful alternatives, www.commonsensemedia.org/tv-reviews/Hotel-Babylon.html.

17. Ben Hirschler, "Internet to Revolutionize TV in 5 Years: Gates," *Reuters*, January 27, 2007.

Chapter 3 Who's Fooling Whom in Cyberspace?

1. C. S. Lewis, *The Screwtape Letters* (New York: Macmillan, 1961), 46.

2. Wendy Koch, *USA Today*, "'Go-getter,' 18, Ousts Mayor in Michigan," November 9, 2005, www.usatoday.com/news/nation/2005-11-09-kid-mayor_x.htm.

3. The official definition of the "rebelution" is "a teenage rebellion against the low expectations of an ungodly culture." Alex and Brett Harris hold conferences around the country to encourage young people to "do hard things." Their website is at www.therebelution.com.

4. The REBELution, www.therebelution.com/blog/2005/11/teens-in-the-news-michael-sessions.

5. Dante Chinni, "Michigan's Kid Mayor: Michael Sessions Is Already the Most Likely to Have Succeeded," *CBS News*, April 3, 2006, www.cbsnews.com/stories/2006/04/03/politics/main1464425_page2.shtml.

6. Francis X. Donnelly, "Hillsdale's Teen Mayor Convicted in Web Prank," *Detroit News*, July 4, 2007, www.detnews.com/apps/pbcs.dll/article?AID=/20070704/METRO/707040365.

7. Tim Jones, "Teen Mayor Facing Pressure," *Chicago Tribune*, July 25, 2007, www.chicagotribune.com/news/nationworld/chi-070725recall,1,364603.story?coll=chi_news_nationworld_util&ctrack=1&cset=true.

8. Donnelly, "Hillsdale's Teen Mayor Convicted in Web Prank."

9. Robert Wilde, "When Did Columbus 'Discover' the Americas?" About.com, http://europeanhistory.about.com/od/colonimperialism/a/dyk4.htm.

10. Columbus Day—A History, http://wilstar.com/holidays/columbus.htm.

11. "French Official Suggested Bush Was behind September 11," *Reuters*, July 7, 2007, www.reuters.com/article/topNews/idUSL0735514520070707.

12. FBI, "Military Names Being Used in E-mail Scams," *Info World*, July 17, 2007, www .infoworld.com/article/07/07/17/FBI-and-military-names-being-used-in-email-scams_1 .html.

13. My Space, www.myspace.com.

14. Andrew Keen, *The Cult of the Amateur* (New York: Currency Books, 2007), 9.

15. Andy Raskin, "How to Lead Your Customer into Temptation," *CNNMoney.com*, May 4, 2006, http://money.cnn.com/magazines/business2/business2_archive /2006/ 05/01/8375932/index.htm.

16. See discussion about age verification on MySpace, CollegeNET Forum, www .collegenet.com/elect/app/app?service=external/Forum&sp=3820.

17. Anne Barnard, "MySpace Agrees to Lead Fight to Stop Sex Predators," *New York Times*, January 15, 2008, www.nytimes.com/2008/01/15/us/15myspace.html?_r=1&oref= slogin.

18. Michael G. Conner, "Internet Addiction and Internet Sex," www.crisiscounseling .com/Articles/InternetAddiction.htm.

19. Carl R. Metzgar, "Don't Fool Yourself," *Pit and Quarry*, October 2004, http://find articles.com/p/articles/mi_m3095/is_4_97/ai_n9771247.

20. Conner, "Internet Addiction and Internet Sex."

21. "AMA Considering Video Game Addiction a Disorder," June 22, 2007, http:// netaddictionrecovery.blogspot.com.

22. Kimberly S. Young, "Internet Addiction: Symptoms, Evaluation, and Treatment," in *Innovations in Clinical Practice*, vol. 17, ed. L. VandeCreek and T. L. Jackson (Sarasota, FL: Professional Resource Press, 1999), www.netaddiction.com/articles/symptoms.htm.

23. Angie Rankman, "Internet Addiction: Caught in the Net," Aphrodite Women's Health, May 15, 2006, www.aphroditewomenshealth.com/news/internet_addiction .shtml.

24. See Wikipedia, http://en.wikipedia.org/wiki/Internet_addiction#_note-5.

25. Hattie Lee, "17% of Youth Addicted to Internet," JLM Pacific Epoch, January 11, 2007, www.pacificepoch.com/newsstories/86510_0_5_0_M.

26. Proverbs 18:24 (NIV).

27. AP, "Ohio Students Accused of Posting Fake Snow-Day Notice on School's Website," *USA Today*, February 10, 2007, www.usatoday.com/news/nation/2007-02-10-fake-snowday_x htm.

28. Nadya Labi, "An IM Infatuation Turned to Romance. Then the Truth Came Out," *Wired*, www.wired.com/print/politics/law/magazine/15-09/ff_internetlies.

29. Ibid.

30. Digital Librarian, www.digital-librarian.com.

31. Michigan eLibrary, www.MEL.org.

32. John Suler, "The Disinhibition Effect," *CyberPsychology and Behavior* 7 (2004): 321–26; also Dr. John Suler's *The Psychology of Cyberspace*, www-usr.rider.edu/~suler/psycyber/ disinhibit.html.

33. Lewis, *Screwtape Letters*, 46.

34. Peter Steiner, in the *New Yorker*, July 5, 1993, www.cartoonbank.com/product_details .asp?sid=22230.

35. The Drudge Report, www.drudgereport.com.

36. The Huffington Post, www.huffingtonpost.com.

37. Psalm 139:2–4 (NIV).

38. Matthew 28:20 (NIV).

Chapter 4 Do the Ends Justify the Means?

1. Jonathan D. Glater, "Cheating Gets Easier with Gadgetry," *International Herald-Tribune*, May 18, 2006, www.iht.com/articles/2006/05/18/technology/web.0518cheat.php.

2. Lori Aratani, "Ethics Boundaries Still Appear Fuzzy," *Washington Post*, November 19, 2006, http://www.washingtonpost.com/wp-dyn/content/article/2006/11/18/AR2006111800888_pf.html.

3. Ibid.

4. David Callahan, *The Cheating Culture* (Orlando: Harcourt, 2004), 14.

5. Wikipedia, "World's Largest Universities," http://en.wikipedia.org/wiki/Mega_university.

6. Jeffrey Selingo, "Is iTunes U for You?" *Washington Post*, November 4, 2007; www.washingtonpost.com/wp-dyn/content/article/2007/10/31/AR2007103102521.html?hpid=topnews.

7. www.graduate.norwich.edu/infoassurance.

8. Kendra Mayfield, "Cheating's Never Been Easier," *Wired*, September 4, 2001, www.wired.com/culture/education/news/2001/09/45803.

9. Secure Computing Corporation, press release, September 7, 2005, www.securecomputing.com/press_releases.cfm?ID=753322.

10. Alan Finder, "34 Duke Business Students Face Discipline for Cheating," *New York Times*, May 1, 2007, www.nytimes.com/2007/05/01/us/01duke.html?_r=1&oref=slogin.

11. See HRN Management Group, News & Views blog, http://www.hrnonline.com/hrnblog/PermaLink,guid,84df4c14-3f5a-40bd-86d2-5f8aededc2eb.aspx.

12. Ian Grayson, "Warning Bells Ring on Fake Degrees," *CNN.com*, World Business section, October 11, 2005, http://edition.cnn.com/2005/BUSINESS/10/10/execed.fakes/index.html.

13. EDUCAUSE is a nonprofit association whose mission is to advance higher education by promoting the intelligent use of information technology. For a .edu domain, see the procedures at www.educause.edu/edudomain/request.asp.

14. www.ftc.gov/bcp/conline/pubs/buspubs/diplomamills.shtm.

15. Online Education Database, http://oedb.org. See also http://oedb.org/library/features/diploma-mills.

16. Baker's Guide to Christian Distance Education, www.bakersguide.com.

17. Bob Rosner, "Online Resumes Risk Plagiarism," Working Wounded column of *Lansing State Journal*, November 19, 2006.

18. Pat Curry, "University Gets Tough on Cheating," www.uga.edu/gm/300/FeatTough.html.

19. Rutgers University Policy on Academic Integrity for Undergraduate and Graduate Students, http://ctaar.rutgers.edu/integrity/policy.html.

20. Ibid.

21. "Plagiarist to Sue University," *BBC News*, May 27, 2004, http://news.bbc.co.uk/2/hi/uk_news/education/3753065.stm.

22. Gregg Keizer, "Grand Jury Indicts Ex-Fresno State Students in Grades-for-Cash Hack," *Computerworld*, November 5, 2007, www.computerworld.com/action/article.do?command=viewArticleBasic&articleId=9045585&source=rss_topic17.

23. Jim Dahlman, "News Flash: Christian College Students Cheat! (But Maybe Less than Others)," *Johnson City* (Tenn.) *Press*, May 12, 2007, posted in The Culture Beat, www.theculturebeat.com/?p=380.

24. Ibid.

25. Valparaiso University, Honor System Web page, www.valpo.edu/student/honor/honor_code.html.

26. Ibid.

27. "Shoebear," Response to Dahlman, "News Flash," June 25, 2007, www.theculture beat.com/?p=380.

28. Character Counts, www.charactercounts.org/pdf/about/FactSheet-JI-0903.pdf.

29. www.charactercounts.org/parenting_for_integrity.html.

30. Sloan Consortium portal, www.sloan-c.org.

31. Center for Academic Integrity at Clemson University, www.academicintegrity.org.

32. University of Maryland, University College Center for Intellectual Property, www .umuc.edu/distance/odell/cip/links_plagiarism.shtml.

33. University of Maryland, Education Technology Outreach Center, www.edtechout reach.umd.edu/resources.html.

34. State University of New York, "Tips for Handling Technology Enhanced Cheating," http://tlt.suny.edu/originaldocumentation/library/cm/cheat.htm.

35. Proverbs 11:1 (NIV).

36. Proverbs 6:16–19 (NIV).

37. Proverbs 10:9 (NIV).

38. James Montgomery Boice, *Psalms*, vol. 2, *Psalms 42–106* (Grand Rapids: Baker Books, 2005), 858.

Chapter 5 Identity Theft and Integrity Theft

1. David F. Wells, *Losing Our Virtue* (Grand Rapids: Eerdmans, 1998), 63.

2. Warner Brothers, *You've Got Mail* website, http://youvegotmail.warnerbros.com.

3. 2007 IDC study, http://internetcommunications.tmcnet.com/topics/enterprise/ articles/6138-idc-email-not-doing-too-well.htm.

4. Messaging Anti-Abuse Working Group, press release, March 8, 2006, www.maawg .org/news/maawg060308.

5. See "Spamalot: Why Laws Have Failed to Stem the Spam," *Times Online*, November 22, 2006, http://technology.timesonline.co.uk/tol/news/tech_and_web/article645851 .ece; or "Reaching a Truce in the Spam War," www.acquireweb.com/market/Truce%20in %20Spam%20War.htm.

6. Frank Washkuch Jr., "Los Angeles Botmaster Pleads Guilty, Faces 60 Years in Prison, $1.75 Million Fine," *SC Magazine*, November 12, 2007, www.scmagazineus.com/Los-Angeles-botmaster-pleads-guilty-faces-60-years-in-prison-175-million-fine/article/96325.

7. "White lists" contain e-mail addresses and other trusted information from vetted sources that we can rely on.

8. Opening Remarks of Deborah Platt Majoras, "Developing a Plan for Action in the Fight against Malicious Spam," Spam Summit: The Next Generation of Threats and Solutions, July 11, 2007, www.ftc.gov/speeches/majoras/070703spamsummit.pdf.

9. FBI press release, "Over 1 Million Potential Victims of Botnet Cyber Crime," June 13, 2007, www.fbi.gov/pressrel/pressrel07/botnet061307.htm.

10. Symantec Threat Report, September 2007, www.symantec.com/business/theme .jsp?themeid=threatreport.

11. Christopher Rhoads, "Web Scammer Targets Senior U.S. Executives," *Wall Street Journal Online*, November 9, 2007, http://online.wsj.com/article/SB119456922698387317 .html?mod=fpa_mostpop.

12. Lisa Vaas, "Attackers Snatch Member Data from 92 Nonprofits," *eWeek Online*, November 12, 2007, www.eweek.com/article2/0,1895,2215792,00.asp.

13. "A Chronology of Data Breaches," Privacy Rights Clearing House, www.privacy rights .org/ar/ChronDataBreaches.htm#2007.

14. See www.Michigan.gov/cybersecurity; also www.Michigan.gov/ag.

15. Brian Krebs, "Be Prepared for ID Theft," *Washington Post*, June 18, 2006.

16. Eric Morath, "ID Theft Added to Home Coverage," *Detroit News*, November 5, 2007, www.detnews.com/apps/pbcs.dll/article?AID=/20071105/BIZ/711050314.

17. Richard Greenfield, quoted in Eric Savitz, "Greenfield Downgrades Warner Music; Believes Digital Music Should Be Free," *Seeking Alpha*, November 1, 2007, www.seekingalpha .com/article/52439-greenfield-downgrades-warner-music-believes-digital-music-should-be-free.

18. Christopher Burgess and Richard Power, "How to Avoid Intellectual Property Theft," *CIO* magazine, July 10, 2006, www.cio.com/article/22837.

19. Steven Malanga, "Yes, Rudy Giuliani Is a Conservative," *City Journal*, Winter 2007, www.city-journal.org/html/17_1_rudy_giuliani.html.

20. Ibid.

21. Habbo Hotel, www.habbo.com/help/index-new.html.

22. BBC News, "'Virtual Theft' Leads to Arrest," November 14, 2007, http://news.bbc .co.uk/2/hi/technology/7094764.stm.

23. Francesca Di Meglio, "Virtual Exchanges Get Real," *Business Week Online*, August 10, 2007, www.businessweek.com/technology/content/aug2007/tc2007089_873900.htm? chan=technology_technology+index+page_top+stories.

24. Wikipedia, http://en.wikipedia.org/wiki/Second_Life.

25. Adam Reuters, "UPDATE 3—Linden Lab Outlaws Second Life Gambling," *Reuters*, July 26, 2007, http://secondlife.reuters.com/stories/2007/07/26/linden-lab-outlaws-second-life-gambling.

26. Rob Hof, "Second Life's First Millionaire," *Business Week*, November 26, 2006, www.businessweek.com/the_thread/techbeat/archives/2006/11/second_lifes_fi.html.

27. Adam Reuters, "IBM Accelerates Push into 3D Virtual Worlds," *Reuters*, November 9, 2006, http://secondlife.reuters.com/stories/2006/11/09/ibm-accelerates-push-into-3d-virtual-worlds.

28. Symantec Internet Security Threat Report, Trends for January to June 2007, http:// eval.symantec.com/mktginfo/enterprise/white_papers/ent-whitepaper_internet_security_ threat_report_xii_exec_summary_09_2007.en-us.pdf.

29. Christy Pettey, "Gartner Says 80 Percent of Active Internet Users Will Have a 'Second Life' in the Virtual World by the End of 2011," Gartner website press release, April 24, 2007, www.gartner.com/it/page.jsp?id=503861.

30. Interview with David O'Berry, director of Information Technology Systems and Services, SC Dept. of Probation, Parole, and Pardon Services, October 30, 2007.

31. US-CERT Reading Room, www.us-cert.gov/reading_room.

32. US-CERT Guide, "Before You Connect a New Computer to the Internet," www .us-cert.gov/reading_room/before_you_plug_in.html.

33. C. S. Lewis, *The Screwtape Letters* (New York: Macmillan, 1961), 56.

34. Ibid., 119.

35. Charles Reader, inspirational quote on habit, http://quotations.about.com/cs/ inspirationquotes/a/Habits1.htm. Also, an ancient Chinese proverb, original source unknown.

36. Steven Curtis Chapman, "Next Five Minutes," www.sing365.com/music/lyric.nsf/Next-Five-Minutes-lyrics-Steven-Curtis-Chapman/D26B514AFAF2B85148 256D7600274153.

Chapter 6 This Is Looking Like Work

1. Charles Haddon Spurgeon, sermon #797, "Spots in Our Feasts of Charity," www .spurgeongems.org/vols13-15/chs797.pdf p7.

2. "Online Oxygen," *Trend Watching Online Newsletter*, www.trendwatching.com/trends/ ONLINE_OXYGEN.htm.

3. Deborah Rothberg, "As Crucial as Coffee: Web Surfing at Work," *eWeek*, www.eweek .com/article2/0,1759,1963997,00.asp.

4. Finfacts Business News Centre, "US Leads World in Labour Productivity," www.finfacts .com/irelandbusinessnews/publish/article_1011022.shtml.

5. Crackberry.com, Tell Us Your CrackBerry Story, http://forums.crackberry.com/ f45/tell-us-your-crackberry-addiction-story-242/.

6. Sylvia Ann Hewlett and Carolyn Buck Luce, "Extreme Jobs: The Dangerous Allure of the 70-Hour Workweek," *Harvard Business Review*, December 2006, www.worklife policy. org/index.php/section/research_pubs.

7. Dominic Rushe, "The Americans Who Are Addicted to Work," *Times*Online (UK), June 10, 2007, http://business.timesonline.co.uk/tol/business/article1909371.ece.

8. William D. Hyatt, sermon, "Work: A Question of Identity," Peninsula Bible Church, Cupertino, California, November 22, 1998, www.pbcc.org/sermons/hyatt/1185.html.

9. Comcast Cable, Triples Language, www.tripleslanguage.com.

10. Helen Leggatt, "Web Surfers' Attention Spans Shortening," *BizReport*, November 7, 2007, www.bizreport.com/2007/11/web_surfers_attention_spans_shortening.html.

11. "How Much Time Do You Waste at Work?" Lifehacker, July 2007, http://lifehacker .com/software/reader-poll/how-much-time-do-you-waste-at-work-283105.php.

12. Eric Weiner, "Use Time Wisely—By Slacking Off," *LA Times*, September 11, 2007, www .latimes.com/news/printedition/opinion/la-oe-weiner11sep11,0,1343248.story?coll=la-news-comment.

13. U.S. Department of Interior audit report, entitled, "Excessive Indulgences," September 2006, www.doioig.gov/upload/FINALInternetreport1.pdf (text version: www .doioig.gov/upload/InternetUsage1.txt).

14. A cyber forensic investigation analyzes computers for deleted files and network traffic that is relevant to a specific case. Just as DNA evidence is left at the scene of a crime, substantial evidence left over from whatever actions were taken often can be found by computer forensic investigations.

15. For more details, see Lohrmann on GovSpace, http://blogs.csoonline.com/node/ 570.

16. See US-CERT study, www.cert.org/insider_threat/docs/insider threatISDC2005 .pdf.

17. "Insider Security Threats: State CIOs Take Action Now!" NASCIO, April 2007, http:// www.nascio.org/publications/documents/NASCIO-InsiderSecurityThreats.pdf.

18. Information from ibid., 3.

19. See www.Sans.org; also documents for Summit on Insider Threats 2007, www .compliancehome.com/events/Basel-II/Conferences/details10607.html.

20. Tom Espiner, "Locating the Real Threats to Corporate Security," *ZDNet*, July 27, 2007, http://resources.zdnet.co.uk/articles/features/0,1000002000,39287839,00.htm.

21. Deborah Gage, "Employees Take Greater Risks at Work than Home," *Baseline*, November 26, 2007, www.baselinemag.com/c/a/Projects-Security/Employees-Take-Greater-Risks-at-Work-Than-Home.

22. Tim Wilson, "End Users Flout Enterprise Security Policies," *Dark Reading*, December 10, 2007, www.darkreading.com/document.asp?doc_id=141002&WT.svl=news2_2.

23. David W. Miller, *God at Work: The History and Promise of the Faith at Work Movement* (Oxford: Oxford University Press, 2006), 9.

24. Deborah Perelman, "What's Your Google Rep?" *eWeek*, November 1, 2007, www .careers.eweek.com/print_article/Whats+Your+Google+Rep/218527.aspx.

25. Paul McDougall, "IBM Issues Employee Conduct Rules for Second Life," *Information Week*, July 27, 2007, www.informationweek.com/news/showArticle.jhtml? articleID=201201541.

26. See Marshall Sponder, "Virtual World Advertising," Web Metrics Guru, December 6, 2007, www.webmetricsguru.com/2007/12/virtual_world_advertising_from.html.

27. "Headscarf Defeat Riles French Muslims," *BBC News*, November 1, 2005, http://news.bbc.co.uk/2/hi/europe/4395934.stm.

28. See Gartner website and reports, "Consumerization: The IT Civil War," www.gartner.com/it/products/research/consumerization_it/consumerization.jsp; Brian Gammage and David Mitchell Smith, "Steps Toward Managed Withdrawal from User Devices at Work," May 14, 2007.

29. See ibid.

30. Cath Everett, "The Dangers of Taking Consumer Tech to Work," *ZDNet UK*, October 29, 2007,http://resources.zdnet.co.uk/articles/features/0,1000002000,39290423-1,00.htm.

31. See Rachael King, "The Good and Bad of Tagalong Technology," *Business Week*, July 16, 2007, http://www.businessweek.com/technology/content/jul2007/tc20070710_432189.htm; also, "KLM: Letting Outside Tech In," www.businessweek.com/technology/content/jul2007/tc20070715_157962.htm.

32. ExaProtect Newsletter, www.exaprotect.com/resources/newsletters.

33. A Google search for "pre-employment tests for integrity" yielded over 55,000 results in December 2007.

34. "Study Debunks Ethics Management Myths," Penn State Smeal College of Business, April 9, 2004, http://live.psu.edu/story/6370p.

35. Word of Mouth Marketing Association (WOMMA) draft ethics code, www.womma.org/ethics/code.

36. www.shrewdenterprise.com/business-ethics.

37. Richard Mbuthia, "Workplace Ethics: Say No to Laziness," www.shrewdenterprise.com/business-ethics/index.php?artid=workplace_ethics_say_no_to_laziness_89.

38. "Workers, Surf at Your Own Risk," *Business Week Online*, June 12, 2000, www.businessweek.com/2000/00_24/b3685257.htm. A sextracker.com report in 2004 reconfirmed this percentage.

Chapter 7 Just Do It

1. Donald L. Caruth and Gail D. Handlogten-Caruth, "A Company's Number One Killer: Procrastination," *Innovative Leader* 12, no. 5 (May 2003), www.winstonbrill.com/bril001/html/article_index/articles/551-600/article577_body.html.

2. See BrainyQuote, www.brainyquote.com/quotes/keywords/main.html.

3. Brian J. Walsh and J. Richard Middleton, *The Transforming Vision* (Downers Grove, IL.: InterVarsity Press, 1984), 32.

4. Jerry Solomon, "Worldviews," Probe Ministries, www.probe.org/theology-and-philosophy/worldview–philosophy/worldviews.html#text3.

5. www.ivotevalues.org.

6. Sample chart of earliest Christian values, www.bibletexts.com/terms/genuine-christianity.htm.

7. Anderson Estwick, "Christian Values: A Key Component in Adventist Technology Programs," Institute for Christian Teaching, 18th International Faith and Learning Seminar, West Indies College, Mandeville, Jamaica, June 16–28, 1996, www.aiias.edu/ict/vol_17/17cc_079-093.htm.

8. Sample chart of earliest Christian values.

9. Seventh-day Adventist Church, South Pacific Curriculum Division, "Business Studies, Seventh-day Adventist Secondary Curriculum Framework, 1998," 21–35, www.aiias.edu/ict/Supplements/Business.htm.

10. Psalm 101:3 (NIV).

11. Psalm 34:1, 14 (NIV).

12. http://www.covenantlife.net/clientImages/9032/Teachings/the_power_of_pa tience.pdf.

13. www.safefamilies.org/safetypledge.php.

14. Edward C. Baig, "Tech Show Tackles What's Appropriate (Or Not) for Kids," *USA Today*, January 9, 2008, www.usatoday.com/tech/columnist/edwardbaig/2008-01-09-CES-sandbox-summit_N.htm.

15. International Council of Online Professionals pledge, http://i-cop.org/pledge .htm.

16. Psalm 101:3 (NIV).

17. Ronald Rolheiser, "Betraying Jesus as Peter Did," *Tidings Online*, March 17, 2006, www.the-tidings.com/2006/0317/rolheiser.htm.

18. See "Study of the Extended Family," Marriage and Family Encyclopedia, http:// family.jrank.org/pages/473/Extended-Families-Study-Extended-Family.html.

19. Project Management Institute, www.pmi.org.

20. Simon Kent, "The Buck Stops Here," in ibid., www.pmi.org/Marketplace/Pages/ ProductDetail.aspx?GMProduct=00100903300.

21. Ross Bonander, "Habits Bosses Love," Career Adviser column, www.Askmen.com, www.askmen.com/money/professional_150/169_professional_life.html.

22. "One 2 One Nutrition," http://one2onenutrition.co.uk/newsletter%20articles/ The-falure-of-one-size-fits-all-approach.htm.

23. Weight Watchers, www.weightwatchers.com/plan/mtg/meetings_work.aspx; also www.weightwatchers.com/util/art/index_art.aspx?art_id=33481&tabnum=1&sc=808& subnav=In+the+Spotlight.

24. "Diet Programs," Epigee Women's Health, www.epigee.org/fitness/diet_programs .html.

25. See www.promisekeepers.org and http://proverbs31.gospelcom.net.

26. D. Martyn Lloyd-Jones, "Sermon—Living the Righteous Life," *Studies in the Sermon on the Mount* (Grand Rapids: Eerdmans, 1984), p. 295.

Chapter 8 Surf Your Values

1. Quoted in Joshua Porter, "Simplicity: The Ultimate Sophistication," User Interface Engineering, April 9, 2007, www.uie.com/articles/simplicity.

2. Dan Lohrmann, "Government Web Sites Must Focus More on the User," *Government Computer News*, June 19, 2000, www.gcn.com/print/vol19_no16/2213-1.html.

3. Steve Jobs, Apple CEO at a user conference, www.37signals.com/svn/archives/000692 .php; also www.simplicityweb.co.uk/simplicity.html.

4. See comments at www.spywaredb.com/remove-covenant-eyes.

5. "Geek Squad" information from Best Buy, www.bestbuy.com/olspage.jsp?id=pcm cat38200050030&type=category.

6. www.OnGuardOnline.gov.

7. Safe Families software analysis, www.safefamilies.org/SoftwareTools.php.

8. *PC Magazine*, www.pcmag.com (see reviews tab).

9. *SC Magazine*, www.scmagazine.com or www.scmagazineus.com/2008-Awards-Finalists/ section/260.

10. www.OnGuardOnline.gov.

11. "Norton Internet Security 2008," Norton, www.symantec.com/norton/products/ overview.jsp?pcid=is&pvid=nis2008.

12. SafeEyes, www.internetsafety.com/safe-eyes.

13. Covenant Eyes, www.covenanteyes.com.

14. X3WatchPro, www.x3watch.com.

15. www.promisekeepers.org/about/faqs/internet/integrity/eyepromise.

16. Covenant Eyes, www.covenanteyes.com.

17. Jim Edwards, "Online Temptation Blocker," July 25, 2006, www.thenetreporter .com.

18. University of Michigan, "Be Aware You're Uploading," www.bayu.umich.edu.

19. Andy Patrizio, "Survey: Most PCs Are Running Out-of-Date Software," Enterprise IT Planet.com, January 14, 2008, www.enterpriseitplanet.com/security/news/article.php/ 3721406.

20. Tips for high-speed Internet connections, www.connectmyhighspeed.com/blog/ connectmyhighspeed.

21. The National Institute on Media and the Family, www.mediafamily.org.

22. Robin Raskin, "Raising Kids Online and Offline: Striking the Right Balance," Raising Digital Kids, September 2004, www.robinraskin.com/blog/your-digital-kids/raising-kids-online-and-offline-striking-the-right-balance/.

23. An Nguyen and Mark Western, "The Complementary Relationship between the Internet and Traditional Mass Media: The Case of Online News and Information," *IR Information Research* 11, no. 3 (April 2006), http://informationr.net/ir/11-3/paper259 .html.

24. Jim Wagner, "Always-Connected, Tech Savvy—and Happy?" Earthweb.com, April 1, 2005, http://itmanagement.earthweb.com/career/article.php/3494746.

25. Paula Eder, "Finding Time by Avoiding Temptation—7 Tips for the Internet," *Successful Business Decision Making,* April 13, 2007, http://successfullbusinessdecisions. blogspot.com/2007/04/finding-time-by-avoiding-temptation-7.html, see also: http:// ezinearticles.com/?expert=Paula_Eder.

26. Jeremy Smith, "Filtering & Accountability Software Roundup," Deeper Devotion, http://deeperdevotion.com/articles/1399.

27. BOB, www.usebob.com.

28. Time Scout monitor, www.time-scout.com.

29. "10 Signs Your Child Is Breaking the Rules Online," InternetSafety.com, www .internetsafety.com/safety-tips/articles/10SignsBreakingRules.php.

30. "Taking Online Relationships Offline Tips" Life Tips, http://relationship.lifetips .com/cat/64856/taking-online-relationships-offline.

31. "Entertainment Topics," Focus on Your Child, www.focusonyourchild.com/entertain /art1.

32. Thomas Wailgum, "Why I'm Just Saying No to Facebook," *CIO,* January 14, 2008, http://advice.cio.com/thomas_wailgum/why_im_just_saying_no_to_facebook?source= nlt_cioinsider.

33. Larry Chase predicts Internet-free vacations, Web Digest for Marketers, www.wdfm .com/trends-internet-marketing.php.

34. "Forest Penetrating Wireless Solution Deployed in Sierra National Forest Yosemite National Park Area Campgrounds," *Broadband Wireless Exchange Magazine,* www.bbwexchange .com/publications/newswires/page546-1086276.asp.

35. Proverbs 11:2 (NIV).

36. Václav Havel, *The Art of the Impossible: Politics as Morality in Practice, Speeches and Writings, 1990–1996,* trans. Paul Wilson (New York: Fromm International, 1998), 30–31.

37. Ibid., 19.

38. Quentin J. Schultze, *Habits of the High-Tech Heart: Living Virtuously in the Information Age* (Grand Rapids: Baker Academic, 2002), 105–6.

39. Abilene Christian University Counseling Center, www.acu.edu/campusoffices/ counseling/Help_and_Healing.html.

40. Virtuous Reality, www.virtuousreality.com.

41. Men of Integrity, www.menofintegrity.org.
42. Freedom Begins Here, www.freedombeginshere.org.
43. Pure Desire Ministries, www.puredesire.org/default.aspx.
44. Ibid.
45. John Piper, *Future Grace* (Minneapolis: Multnomah, 2005).
46. Ibid.
47. John Piper, "Anthem: Strategies for Fighting Lust," November 5, 2001, Desiring God, www.desiringgod.org/ResourceLibrary/TasteAndSee/ByDate/2001/1187_A_N_T_H_E_M.
48. Josephson Institute Business Ethics Center, www.josephsoninstitute.org/business-ethics.html.
49. John 18:37 (NIV).
50. John 14:6 (NIV).
51. Proverbs 3:5–6 (NIV).
52. Matt 10:32–33 (NIV).
53. James 4:6 (NIV).
54. Redeemer Presbyterian Church in New York City, "The Gospel: The Key to Change—Vision Paper #1" www.redeemer2.com/visioncampaign/papers/Vision_Paper_1-The_Gospel-The_Key_to_Change.pdf.
55. Redeemer Presbyterian Church in New York City, "Christians and Culture—Vision Paper #6," www.redeemer2.com/visioncampaign/papers/Vision_Paper_6-Christians_and_Culture.pdf.
56. Michael Wittmer, *Heaven Is a Place on Earth: Why Everything You Do Matters to God* (Grand Rapids: Zondervan, 2004), 199.
57. See Redeemer Store, http://sermons.redeemer.com/store/index.cfm; or see Desiring God, www.desiringgod.org/ResourceLibrary.
58. Center for a Christian Worldview, http://grts.cornerstone.edu/resources/llc/resources/ccwstatement/.
59. Ford Motor Company website for teen driver safety, www.drivingskillsforlife.com.
60. BRAVEheart, www.braveheart.org.
61. Robert Wilensky, www.quotedb.com/quotes/2898.
62. Schultze, *Habits of the High-Tech Heart*, 24.

Chapter 9 What If?

1. Glenn Haussman, "HITEC Offers Future Hotel Tech Glimpse," June 27, 2007, www.hotelinteractive.com/hi_articles.asp?func=print&article_id=8039.
2. Scott van Hartesvelt, president of gCommerce, quoted in ibid.
3. Matthew 5:14–16 (NRSV).
4. Tom R. Halfhill, "XML: The Next Big Thing," http://domino.research.ibm.com/comm/wwwr_thinkresearch.nsf/pages/xml199.html.
5. "Google's Goal: To Organise Your Daily Life," *Financial Times*, May 22, 2007, www.ft.com/cms/s/c3e49548-088e-11dc-b11e-000b5df10621.html.
6. Remarks by Steve Ballmer, PC Forum, Scottsdale, Arizona, March 14, 2000, www.microsoft.com/presspass/exec/steve/03-14pcforum.mspx.
7. Net neutrality is a debate over laws determining whether Internet traffic can be given preferential treatment. "The neutrality issue pits large broadband providers such as AT&T, Comcast, and Verizon against consumer groups and large Internet-based companies such as Amazon.com, eBay, and Google. A neutrality law would create new regulations for the Internet, broadband providers say. They argue that they need to explore new business plans as a way to pay for next-generation broadband networks, and that they should be free to divide up their broadband pipes to offer new services such as television over IP."

See Grant Gross, "Battle Lines Drawn over Net Neutrality," *InfoWorld*, July 7, 2006, www .infoworld.com/article/06/07/07/28NNnetneutral_1.html.

See also "Ron Paul Softens Stance on Net Neutrality; Talks on Other Tech Issues," Tech Crunch, January 29, 2008; www.techcrunch.com/2008/01/29/ron-paul-softens-stance-on-net-neutrality-talks-on-other-tech-issues.

8. Web search market share for January 2008, http://marketshare.hitslink.com/report .aspx?qprid=4.

9. ABC News Australia, "Conroy Announces Mandatory Internet Filters to Protect Children," December 31, 2007, www.abc.net.au/news/stories/2007/12/31/2129471.htm.

10. MSNBC.com, "75 percent of Americans overweight by 2015," *Reuters*, July 19, 2007, www.msnbc.msn.com/id/19845784.

11. Kellogg Company, press release, June 14, 2007, www.kelloggcompany.com/uploaded Files/KelloggCompany/Home/Press%20Release%20-%20U%20S.pdf.

Chapter 10 Brave New Web

1. www.sony.com.

2. "Google's Andy Rubin, Discusses the Company's Cell Phone Strategy," *USA Today*, November 11, 2007, www.usatoday.com/tech/wireless/phones/2007-11-05-google-cell phone-qa_N.htm.

3. "U.S. High Court Rejects Decency Act, but Questions Loom over Net Access in Homes, Libraries," *Information Outlook*, September 1997, http://findarticles.com/p/ articles/mi_m0FWE/is_n9_v1/ai_20152133.

4. Dinesh D'Souza, *The Enemy at Home* (New York: Doubleday, 2007), 116–17.

5. www.christianet.com.

6. The High Calling of Our Daily Work, www.thehighcalling.org.

7. Faith In the Workplace, www.FaithInTheWorkplace.com.

8. Plugged In Online, www.pluggedinonline.com.

9. Christian social networking, www.xianz.com.

10. Lights Together, www.LightsTogether.com.

11. See Marguerite Reardon, "10 Things Your Phone Will Do in 10 Years," *CNET.com*, www.cnet.com/4520-13387_1-6737990-1.html.

12. Adam Jackson, "What a Free Cell Phone Service Might Look Like," www.jackson found.com/2007/06/06/what-a-free-cell-phone-service-might-look-like.

13. Daksh Sharma, "Motorola Recognizes the Power of Social Networking," Rev2.org, November 16, 2007, www.rev2.org/2007/11/16/motorola-recognizes-the-power-of-social-networking.

14. Zachary Rodgers, "ISPs Collect User Data for Behavioral Ad Targeting," ClickZ Network, January 3, 2008, www.clickz.com/showPage.html?page=3628004.

15. Zachary Rodgers, "FTC Proposes Self-Regulation Rules for Behavioral Ad Players," ClickZ Network, December 20, 2007, www.clickz.com/showPage.html?page=3627950.

16. See "Finding Loyal Customers in Cyberspace," www.practicalecommerce.com/ articles/185/Finding-Loyal-Customers-in-Cyberspace.

17. Liz Montalbano, "Building Brands in Cyberspace," www.robfrankel.com/phoneplus .html.

18. Philippians 4:8–9 (NIV).

Appendix Toward a New National Strategy on Cyber Ethics

1. John Paul II, "Veritatis Splendor," commenting on the risk of alliance between democracy and ethical relativism, "Pope: True Democracy Is Not 'Truth' by Majority Vote," LifeSite News, February 25, 2000, www.lifesite.net/ldn/2000/feb/00022501.html.

2. Executive summary, President's Task Force on Identity Theft, *Combating ID Theft: A Strategic Plan,* www.idtheft.gov/reports/StrategicPlan.pdf, p. 11.

3. Ibid.

4. C. G. Lynch, "This Is Not a Game: Virtual Worlds Coming to Your Business, Forrester Predicts," *CIO,* January 9, 2008, www.cio.com/article/170850.

5. CPSR—Computer Professionals for Social Responsibility, "What Is Participatory Design?" www.cpsr.org/issues/pd/introInfo.

6. Richard MacManus, "Web 2.0 for Designers," *Digital Web Magazine,* May 4, 2005, www.digital-web.com/articles/web_2_for_designers.

7. Alexis Christoforous, "Companies Rewarding Workers' Healthy Habits," *CBS News,* January 2, 2008, http://wcbstv.com/business/corporations.combat.obesity.2.621317.html.

8. Safe Communities, www.safecommunitycoalition.net; Learning Family, www.learningfamily.net/about/values.htm.

9. Kaiser Family Foundation, "Parents, Children and Media Guide," June 2007, www.kff.org/entmedia/upload/7638.pdf.

10. www.oikoumene.org/?id=3606.

11. www.cc.org/joinfbtf.cfm.

12. www.wabashcenter.wabash.edu/home/default.aspx.

13. http://ikeepsafe.org.

14. Neela Banerjee, "New Coalition of Christians Seeks Changes at Borders," *New York Times,* May 8, 2007, http://www.nytimes.com/2007/05/08/washington/ 08immigration.html?_r=2&adxnnl=1&oref=slogin&ref=us&adxnnlx=1198588449-HPrzHiw53keg8aljSumiHg&oref=slogin.

15. www.charactercounts.org.

16. www.socratesinstitute.org/curriculum/cyberethics.html.

17. www.staysafeonline.org/basics/educators.html.

18. Michael Rubinkam, "Cell Porn Scandal Hits Pa. High School," January 24, 2008, http://ap.google.com/article/ALeqM5jQGRI2CCYKYhT5Iv_ka7uDenhPUgD8UCJ6QO3.

19. Tools for Teaching Cyber Ethics, Education World, www.educationworld.com/a_tech/tech/tech055.shtml.

20. Computer Ethics Institute, a project of the Brookings Institution, *Ten Commandments of Computer Ethics,* www.brook.edu/its/cei/cei_hp.htm.

21. http://connect.educause.edu/browse/645?time=1201566072.

22. Axiom TV, www.axiom.tv.

23. www.dove.org/aboutdove.asp?ArticleID=36.

24. ABC News Australia, "Conroy Announces Mandatory Internet Filters to Protect Children," www.abc.net.au/news/stories/2007/12/31/2129471.htm.

3 5282 00668 8744